PRAISE FOR
POWER OVER STRESS

*"A brilliant, practical approach to mastering everyday stress.
Highly recommended. Run, don't walk, to get your copy."*

—JOY BRAMBLE, *Publisher,* The Baltimore Times

*"Dr Nedd has turned his spellbinding oratory into a brilliant
book on stress. Here are 35 simple, practical prescripions that
can drastically improve the quality of your life."*

—ART VERTLIEB, QC,
Governor, Association of Trial Lawyers of America

THE
TIME
TO BE
HAPPY
IS
NOW

KENFORD NEDD, M.D.

52 Quick Prescriptions for
Bringing Happiness into Your Life

QP PRESS
TORONTO, CANADA

Library and Archives Canada Cataloguing in Publication

Nedd, Kenford
The time to be happy is now : 52 quick prescriptions for bringing happiness into your life / Kenford Nedd.

ISBN 978-0-9733291-1-7

1. Happiness. I. Title.
BF575.H27N43 2008   152.4'2   C2008-900576-7

Design and production supervision: *Mad Dog Design Connection Inc.*
Printed in Canada by *Webcom*

For information concerning the purchase of additional copies of this book, please contact:

Dr. Kenford Nedd at info@stressdoctors.com or telephone 604.632.9500

This book is dedicated to a mentor:

*The Right Honorable Sir Allan F. L. Louisy,
retired Supreme Court Judge and former
Prime Minister of St Lucia.*

*Sir Allan, thank you for helping so many people
in their struggle to find happiness. You have shown
us all how to live a victorious life full of love
and kindness in all circumstances.*

ACKNOWLEDGEMENT

I am very grateful for all the assistance and advice
I received from one of the best book designers in the
business, Linda Pellowe of Mad Dog Design. I also would
like to thank Pamela Erlichman for her help and patience in
the preparation of the manuscript and all my patients who
have taught me so much over the years.

I would also like to thank my family, Mariela, Kaiyo, Keymo
and Kara for their encouragement and help.

CONTENTS

INTRODUCTION

AN ASTONISHING 80 PERCENT OF MY PATIENTS report that they are unhappy. Unhappiness is rampant, and we don't seem to care too much about it unless the condition becomes acutely unbearable. We take note of painful grief or major depression. We run to the doctor and ask for help when our symptoms are severe enough to be called depression, but we pay little attention to the fact that we are, for the most part, unhappy in the daily conduct of our lives.

We tend to accept our unhappiness, as if this were the natural order of things. Even if we wanted to change our state, we seem to lack the skill and internal strength necessary to create the happiness in our lives that we really crave.

Those who are suffering from clinical depression can be treated with drugs, such as Paxil or Elavil, but those of us who are just plain unhappy have fewer options. There is no temple to frequent that is devoted to the cure for unhappiness, no physician who can heal the broken-hearted, no pill that can produce life satisfaction. We may engage in behaviors that bring us pleasure, but we know very little about how to create happiness.

My 18-year-old daughter was flying from Seattle to Boston. When she reached the check-in counter, she suddenly realized that she had forgotten to bring with her two magazines she had planned to read during the flight. She became very upset and started musing, "What am I going to do for five hours without my reading material? I have no computer, no games and no crossword puzzle. What am I going to do? How will I survive this trip? I must find a magazine in this airport somewhere." And with that, she rushed off to a bookstore in search of something pleasing to read, and nearly missed her flight. She just did not know how to make herself happy for five hours without a little help from a magazine.

How do you make yourself happy? That is the question we will try to answer in this book. We have the technology! Together we will explore a variety of practical techniques that have the power to create and sustain a feeling of happiness through thick and thin.

The 52 Quick Prescriptions in this book, one for every weeek of the year, are remedies that will bring you happiness and good health—the time to be happy is now! My hope is that you will select a few of these quick tips and prescriptions to use on a continuing basis to help you raise the level of happiness in your life. After all, your happiness is in your hands and yours alone.

Happiness begins with a decision.

However disruptive your circumstances, however depressed and in pain you feel, embrace the decision that you are going to become a truly happy person. Hold this thought securely through all the changing times of your life.

REMEMBER THIS: THE TIME TO BE HAPPY IS NOW

DAY AFTER DAY IN MY OFFICE, I see patients who seem to have everything yet who are downright miserable.

Ralph is a tall, handsome, wealthy man who is in excellent physical health. He owns several high-rise apartment buildings in the best section of one of the most beautiful cities in the world, and he has the respect and admiration of his community. In his leisure, he travels around the world, playing tennis whenever he wants, with a retinue of rich friends. When he is in town, he spends at least an hour a day walking through one of the most beautiful parks in the world.

Despite all this, Ralph is a miserable, pathetic creature who drags himself into my medical center every week in a state of abject joylessness. He describes himself as empty and tells me that he would give anything for an ounce of happiness in his life. The great mystery is that Ralph has everything the average person wants, yet he is the most miserable patient I have ever had.

Ralph exemplifies the truism that neither material things nor other people's praise and admiration can make you a happy person. He has made me realize that happiness is the big prize in life and it is something that only you can give to yourself.

I hope I can convince you to embrace the concept that you are on this earth to be happy. I want you to think of happiness as the natural order of things. Without happiness, life is hardly worth living. In other words, feeling good is what being here is all about.

If you feel unhappy most of the time, you are missing the point.

If you have lots of money, a great career, a wonderful love relationship, and a multitude of friends, and you still don't feel happy, no one in his or her right mind would call you a winner.

The first step to creating a more vibrant and joyful life involves taking a good look at yourself. If you are serious about becoming a happier person, it is important to take a moment and see where you are in your life right now.

QuickTips

Happiness is growth. Take a hard look at yourself. The ability to see yourself as you really are is a crucial part of becoming a happier person. Socrates said the unexamined life is not worth living. Don't be easy on yourself. It takes guts to change and grow, but that is what happiness is.

To get started, jot down answers to these questions:

1 Do I have a pretty good understanding of who I am?

2 Would my family and close friends say I am a happy person?

3 Do I have specific written goals for my life that I contemplate on a daily basis?

4 Do I know what my gifts and talents are?

5 Do I feel good about myself?

6 Do I like my life and the way I spend my time?

7 Am I excited about the work I do every day?

8 Do I know the values and principles that govern my life?

9 Do I live consciously with delicate awareness of the moments of life?

10 Do I take time out to think about how I can improve the quality of my life?

The good news is that you can turn your life around. You can absolutely create the happiness that eludes you. There is a law of physics that says that a body in a certain state will continue to be in that state unless acted upon by a specific force. This is true of human beings. We will continue to be the way we are unless some force persuades us to wake up and change. This need not be a great disaster or overpowering event. The force that triggers a monumental life change could be a casual word from a friend. Even an activity as simple as reading this book can serve as a wake-up call to a happier life.

I hope you will recognize in a new and poignant way that life is going by quickly and that THE TIME TO BE HAPPY IS NOW. If you have not already done so, make the decision right now to become a truly happy person. Happiness begins with a decision.

Through my work as a physician, I have come to believe that one of the root causes of unhappiness is lack of awareness. If we brought a higher level of consciousness to the details of our lives, we would become happier people. A crucial step to a happier life is to pay attention. The importance of focused attention will be emphasized over and over in this book. The fact is that attention leads to control, and we are happy to the degree to which we perceive that we are in control of things.

Develop a keen sense of receptivity to any sensual stimulus. Just begin to notice more things inside and outside yourself.

R̲x̲   Quick Prescription 1

- *Remember that happiness is the big prize in life.*
- *Focus on feeling good. It is what being here is all about.*
- *Tell yourself that the time to be happy is now.*
- *Decide to become a happier person.*
- *Raise the level of your awareness and pay attention to your inner promptings.*

ARE YOU READY
FOR HAPPINESS?

Some people are not ready to be happy yet. They are busy rocketing their way up to one last level of management. Some need to wallow in the familiar pool of anger and resentment a little longer, or hold on to the last strand of guilt for one more day, or feel the venom of hostility and revenge surging through their bodies for another month.

They are just not ready to give it all up and risk being happy. The prison of misery, hard as it is, has a way of protecting you from the unknown bliss that is your true birthright.

Ask yourself, "What is it that is standing in the way of my happiness? What am I holding onto, which if I release, will bring me closer to becoming a happier person?"

2

ASK YOURSELF, "WHO AM I AND WHAT AM I DOING HERE?"

IF YOU REALLY WANT TO BE A HAPPIER PERSON, start by getting to know yourself better. A great way to get to know yourself is to spend time in solitude every day, looking at yourself and examining the way you live your life. Imagine that you are in a helicopter looking down on yourself as you go through your day, and see what you think.

Going into solitude is a tall order for most people. If you are a busy parent, a stressed-out manager, an overworked secretary, or an ambitious student, where are you going to find the time every day to go into solitude? And yet Blaise Pascal, the famous French philosopher, said that all of our troubles as human beings stem from our refusal to spend time alone. Socrates went so far as to say that the unexamined life is not worth living.

So, adopt the philosophy that personal solitude is a must. The trick is to establish a specific time for solitude every day, if only for five minutes. For some people, this might be as soon as they wake up, or before they fall asleep at night, or as part of their lunch break on a park bench.

Make this a part of your daily routine as definite as brushing your teeth or eating breakfast. You will soon experience a profound difference in your level of happiness as you begin to look forward to spending quality time with yourself every day. Don't let a day pass without giving yourself this invaluable gift of spending five minutes in solitude.

If you do honor this commitment to spend time in solitude on a daily basis, you will build a strong foundation for a happier life. Take the time out, but when you do, don't use the time to sit and worry about all the important things you could be doing. Recognize your time in solitude as an important part of your day, and use it well to get to know the grandeur that is within you.

QuickTips

Take time to go into silence and quietly and intentionally focus your awareness on different parts of your body. Silence and the ability to focus your awareness are powerful tools for creating a healthy body and mind.

When you retreat in silence there are four things you can do to make the time productive. You can **R**elax, **R**eflect, be **S**till, and lastly deepen your sense of **P**urpose. Use the acronym **RRSP** to remember.

1 **Relax.** Relaxation is a specific discipline that strengthens your body and mind, and provides the right environment for confidence, courage, and inner strength to flourish. Just sit or lie comfortably by yourself. Shake your arms and legs in tremulous movements for a few moments. Breathe deeply and evenly for a few minutes, allowing all your muscles to go loose and limp. Continue to breathe deeply and focus on your arms and legs, letting them become heavy and warm. Concentrate on your arms and legs while entertaining the words heavy and warm in your mind. A deep sweet sense of peaceful rest and readiness for anything will invade your body. You will feel energized, alert and well rested at the same time, and the more frequently you do this exercise, the more profound the benefits will be.

2 **Reflect.** This is your second assignment. As you continue to relax and breathe deeply, begin to reflect on your experience and on

what you are feeling. Reflection gives significance to your experience. It turns knowledge into wisdom. So, for a moment, reflect on your past, on your values and on what others have said about you, so that you may know yourself more deeply. Try and get a handle on what is going on deep inside your psyche. Ask yourself: "What are my shortcomings? What are my strong points? How can I change for the better? How can I create a more fulfilling life?" Ponder these questions day after day and your happiness will grow.

3 **Be Still.** This is the golden part of the process. This is when you silence your inner voice and just listen. Silence has the power to transform. Silence is the ingredient from which greatness is made. Pretend to reach inside your head and turn off the radio inside. Just focus your attention wholeheartedly on experiencing the impulses and insights arising from deep within your soul.

4 **Develop a Deep Sense of Purpose.** The final step in solitude is to discover your purpose for living and align yourself with it. Many great thinkers have advised us to adopt the belief that we are on the planet for a specific purpose. By taking time in solitude, you can uncover your purpose. This is the time to ask those odd-sounding philosophical questions, "Who am I?" and "What am I doing here?" Do not expect any answers immediately. Just keep asking the questions and keep living your life with the questions in mind and, one day, you will find yourself living the answers. You will have discovered your purpose, and you will be living it.

R Quick Prescription 2

- *Start by knowing yourself better.*
- *Spend five minutes in solitude every day.*
- *Reflect. Ask yourself: "Who am I? What am I doing here?"*
- *Be still. Silence is an important ingredient of a great life.*

THE HAPPINESS
FLOW CHART

Happiness begins with self-awareness, it continues with self-examination, and it matures with the steady unfolding of a deep sense of purpose for your life.

3

RECOGNIZE THE IMPORTANCE OF FEELINGS

IF YOU HAVE A GREAT INCOME, a loving spouse, wonderful children, a fat bank account, and lots of toys, and still do not feel good inside, you are not a winner. Even if you have achieved great and worthy goals, if you do not feel good about yourself and your life, you are a loser. Feeling good is one of the most important parts of being alive, and we should try to capture this feeling as often as possible and hold onto it for as long as possible.

In a busy and productive life, feelings often end up at the bottom of our priority list. We are so obsessed with getting a promotion, helping our children to get a scholarship, or buying a bigger home that we forget how we feel. And years later, when we are old and gray, we realize that we have not really enjoyed the journey of life. We did not feel good.

This is why it is so important to develop the ability to generate good feelings as you live—at home, in the community, and at work. Wherever you are and whatever you are doing, develop a way to remind yourself to entertain good feelings within your body and your mind. Even if you are in trouble, try to generate good feelings. You will think more clearly. You will fare better.

One way to generate good feelings is to make excellence a way of life for yourself. Put a stamp of excellence on everything you do. Bring your own style to bear upon every situation, every task, and do it with elegance. In other words, whatever you do, add a touch of class to it. Do it with extraordinary pride, thought, and devotion; you will feel lifted up, and the good feelings that you experience as a consequence of your actions will add to the overall happiness of your life.

The main criterion for being a winner in life is to be happy. The difference between winners and losers lies not so much in what the winners have, but in what they do not have. Winners do not have the barriers, the doubts, the negative beliefs, and the mental impediments that block their success and frustrate their feelings. They are not weighed down by all the baggage that many of us hold onto—winners travel light. They exude an aura of freedom, and they feel good about themselves and about life in general.

If you want to cultivate one of the basic characteristics of a winner, begin by seeing not what you can gain but what you can lose. Lose the feelings of irritations, hostility, and hate that creep into your soul in response to obnoxious people and difficult situations. Lose the continuous preoccupation with negative thoughts and the dreadful feeling of urgency that stand in the way of your happiness. Keep losing anything that you perceive as the enemy of your good feelings.

Learn to cultivate happiness. Generate happy feelings wherever you are. Try to feel good every moment of every day that you can. Make it a goal to feel good even in the midst of trouble. If you feel good, you will become stronger and your performance in every arena of life will be superior.

As a family doctor, I can tell you that there is nothing more health-enhancing than feelings of happiness flowing constantly through the psycho-physiological system. I believe that the single most important factor that will determine how long you will live is how happy you are. A happy disposition is a strong defense against sicknesses such as cancer, heart disease, and respiratory infections.

Decide now that you are going to generate and embrace happy feelings. Assume such a positive and peaceful attitude that disease and stress will not easily find you. The way to build hardiness against stress, disease, and the vicissitudes of life is to make happy feelings an integral part of everything you do. Put such a thick shield of happiness around you that stress and illness will not be able to penetrate.

I have had the good fortune of treating many patients who reported great happiness in the face of a chronic illness. They understood that happiness is a decision, and they made the decision to generate and entertain happy feelings on a continuing basis. They just decided to feel good about whatever it was that they were experiencing, and they reflected feelings of joy and excitement to everyone. People in turn sent back the good feelings, and happiness was compounded.

How can you create happiness out of nothing? How can you be happy when you don't have enough money to buy the things you want, or when you are burdened with too many important things to do?

You have to open yourself to the realization that happiness can be manufactured. You have to believe that you can use your brain to turn your body into a factory of happy feelings.

- Look at your right hand right now.
- Decide to feel good about your right hand.
- Feel grateful for the advantages that your right hand brings to your life.
- In a few moments, you should begin to notice a strange transformation taking place.

QuickTips

Attention leads to control and control leads to happiness. Turn up the level of your attention and you turn up the level of your happiness. Ignorance is not bliss.

Refuse to believe that happiness is an offshoot of the external environment. Happiness does not come from changing the outside. According to John Powell, happiness is an inside job. Whether you are happy or not depends on your willingness to be challenged by the negative experiences that come your way.

You must fill your mind with hope and optimism in the face of adversity. Foster thoughts such as "Great things are going to happen to me" or "This predicament is a prelude to something wonderful and I must learn from it." Remember, it's your mind. You can fill it with whatever you like.

As a doctor who treats patients with painful disorders every day, this is a hard thing for me to say, but I believe that you can choose your feelings to a great extent, even in the midst of disaster.

Resolve now that you are going to embrace happy feelings, even when your world is upside down.

Quick Prescription 3

- *When you notice that you are unhappy, change your appearance.*
- *Try to look your best and perform all your tasks with a touch of elegance.*
- *Dress to kill on a day that you feel lousy. Put on that suit that you have been saving for a special occasion, polish your shoes, iron your shirt, get a great haircut, and stand tall. Walk as if you are on top of the world.*
- *Arrange it so that you look as good as you possibly can.*
- *When you look good you tend to feel good.*
- *And feeling good is good for you.*

BOOST YOUR LEVEL OF HAPPINESS

Learn to summon happy feelings from the memory of a past experience—a child's hug, the sound of music, or a day at the beach.

Believe that happiness is something you can generate from inside. Don't wait for circumstances to change.

Try always to adopt a happy attitude. Your attitude comes from your thoughts, so think about happy things, especially when the challenges of life overwhelm you.

Pay attention to happy feelings when they appear for no reason. Welcome them. Accentuate them and let them influence the way you carry your face and the way you act.

Try to make other people happy at every opportunity. Ask yourself, "What can I do to make someone especially happy today?" and take action. Making others happy is a noble mission. Besides, the feelings of happiness that you send to others will boomerang right back to you.

Cont'd . . .

Cont'd:

*Don't leave your happiness to chance.
Do something on a continuing basis to make
it a pulsating reality. Surround yourself with
positive people who support you and beware
of those who always seem intent on
bringing you down.*

*Learn to appreciate the simple yet captivating
aspects of life, like a walk in the park, a
beautiful sunset, the sound of rain falling
or the fresh scent of spring.*

*Don't be a victim of emotions. Decide how
you want to feel and go to work to
create those feelings.*

Put a stamp of excellence on everything you do.

*Use any free or boring moment to practice
producing happy feelings in your body and
mind. Do it right now just for the heck of it.*

4

CHANGE THE WAY YOU ACT
AND YOU WILL CHANGE
THE WAY YOU FEEL

THE AMAZING THING about the human condition is that, at any point in our lives, we can decide that we are going to be happy. We can begin then and there to create happiness.

First, always ask yourself if the way you are sitting or standing might be generating tension or blocking the flow of pleasant sensations and impulses in your body?

Are you experiencing any unhappiness because of the way you are responding to negative people or circumstances in your life? Are you allowing yourself to be drawn into the circle of negativity, anxiety, or resentment that is around you? Are you paying too much attention to what is wrong in your life rather than to what is right?

Read these questions again as you examine yourself and get ready to release negativity.

Refuse to let anyone or anything block the flow of positive emotions in your body and mind. Don't give anyone or anything that degree of control over your life.

Ask yourself: "If I were happy, how would I feel? How would I act? What would I be thinking about? How would I talk to my spouse or my friends? What would my face look like?" Imagine what you would be doing or how you would be behaving if you were happy, and begin to act that way.

Even if you feel miserable, act with great appreciation for the gift of life. Be grateful for all the good things in and around you, and let that be the focus of your attention. Be grateful that your eyes are on your face and not on the inside of your right knee.

Induce happy feelings with your thoughts and your attitudes. And when the happy feelings that you summon appear, welcome them with open arms. Pay attention to them and they will stay and expand in your life.

We all have a strong desire to be happy, but the desire is where it stops for most of us. We are not prepared to do the inner work that will produce happiness. If you are serious about being a happy person, let that deep desire for happiness guide you to think and act as if you were already happy.

Imagine how you would feel and how you would be on the inside if you were the happiest person in the world. This is how you shift gears. When you assume the role of a happy person, you take on the posture of a happy person, and the feelings tend to follow.

QuickTips

- **Adopt perfect posture—be balanced, even, and relaxed, head high, neck long, chest open, and eyes looking slightly upwards.**
- **Relax your shoulders by physically adjusting your muscles.**
- **Walk on the balls of your feet, keeping hands a few inches away from your hips.**
- **Keep your posture loose but erect.**
- **Put a smile on your face and let it permeate your whole body.**
- **Breathe deeply and evenly with penetrating awareness.**

Practicing this technique can result in a change in emotions that you feel and in the way your body functions.

Whenever you find yourself getting even a little bit sad, take notice. Be quick to recognize how you feel in all areas of your body and mind. Be a feeler of your feelings.

Notice the way you are carrying your body. Pay attention to the slightest whispers of unhappiness and tension, and, before they take root, take action to eliminate them.

Learn to notice how you are. Simply notice. Then just as quickly as you notice a negative thought, feeling, or attitude, begin to act out the positive opposite.

Refuse to be a container of negative feelings. People who are happy let go of negative feelings and embrace positive ones. It is not just the way they are—it is a conscious decision, an act of will.

I have noticed that happy people tend to dress more attractively and act more enthusiastically. They tend to look upwards, while unhappy people tend to look downwards. Happy people are more apt to smile, even under trying circumstances, while unhappy people may frown and grumble much of the time.

The people who report that they are happy tend to set themselves up for happiness by their own thoughts, words, attitudes, and actions. No wonder happy feelings tend to follow them around. Happiness is indeed a choice.

R℞ Quick Prescription 4

- *Right now commit yourself to becoming a truly happy person.*
- *Act as if you were happy. Think as if you were happy. Treat others as if you were happy.*
- *Pay attention to happiness whenever you notice it in yourself or in others.*

It's so easy to be pleasant

When life flows by like a song,

*But the one who's worthwhile is
the one who will smile,*

When everything goes dead wrong.

For the test of the heart is trouble,

And it always comes with the years,

And the smile that is worth the praises of earth,

Is the smile that shines through the tears.

—Jo Petty from *Apples of Gold*

5
UNLEASH THE SECRET POWER
OF MUSIC AND LAUGHTER

SINCE I STARTED USING MUSIC as a form of treatment in my office, I enjoy my practice much more. Every day, I see the evidence that music has the power to change physiology. Some types of music can energize you and some can make you happy and elated. Some can soothe you, and some can even depress you. I am always amazed at the powerful effect that music has on the body. Different sound waves affect the cell membranes differently and so produce different physiological and psychological states.

I encourage my patients to take advantage of the effects of music by making a 15-minute tape of music that they know makes them feel happy and energized. Playing your own tapes of special music throughout the day will help to make you feel happy and energetic.

Similarly, looking at beautiful things and touching or smelling pleasant things can affect the cells of the body and promote positive feelings. No wonder we are inclined to feel better when we dress well, look sharp, and smell nice.

Why do we tend to feel happy when good things happen to us? When we are surrounded by pleasant views, beautiful music, and nice people we get a sensation of pleasure. Because of these pleasant bodily sensations that originate outside ourselves we are more likely to smile, sing a happy song, play happy music, or act in happy ways. When we behave like this, the feelings of pleasure intensify. This makes us smile more widely, sing more joyfully, whistle more enthusiastically, and act more happily. Before we know it, our emotions are profoundly affected and we are transformed into a truly happy state, not so much because of our fortunate circumstances, but because we changed our attitude and our behavior. Singing, smiling, humming happy music, and behaving cheerfully are what really produce positive emotions. External things, like fine clothes or good news, are simply agents to promote the right attitude to produce the corresponding chemistry in the body.

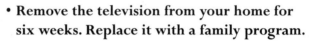

QuickTips

- **Remove the television from your home for six weeks. Replace it with a family program.**
- **Get together to sing songs and tell stories. Play musical instruments or word games.**
- **At the end of six weeks ask yourself if everyone is happier. It's your life. Take a chance at improving it.**

Laughing is a marvelous technique to induce feelings of happiness whenever we want. It can change not only our mood or our perspective but also the way the cells of the brain and body function. When you laugh, several things happen: the blood at the base of the lungs becomes more oxygenated, so that more oxygen-rich blood goes to the brain; this stimulates the neuronal networks that make you think more effectively. So you can literally propel yourself into a different state of mind with the help of laughter, just as you can with the help of music.

Norman Cousins is reported to have cured himself of a serious disease by locking himself in a hotel room and engaging in a heavy dose of laughter all day long for several weeks. I heard that movie star Steve Martin—who has made a string of successful comedies—

routinely spends four minutes laughing every morning. Laughing stimulates creativity.

It is easy to laugh, play happy music, or smile when things are going well. We all do that. But the prize goes to the man or woman who is able to laugh, play happy music, sing, or smile when things are bad. We need to learn to do these things not in reaction to what is happening around us, but as a conscious decision to produce the feelings that we want to experience. The amazing good fortune is that these techniques are entirely under our control and can be initiated any time we want.

R̟ Quick Prescription 5

- *Put together a 15-minute tape of music that makes you feel happy and energized. Play it several times throughout the day.*

- *When you are feeling low, rent two of the funniest movies that you can find and laugh out loud. In this way you can propel yourself into a different state of mind.*

- *Consciously make the decision to change your feelings by smiling, laughing, or playing happy music and being really nice to everyone within your reach.*

ALONG THE ROAD

I walked a mile with Pleasure,

She chatted all the way;

But left me none the wiser,

For all she had to say.

I walked a mile with Sorrow

And ne'er a word said she;

But, oh, the things I learned from her,

When Sorrow walked with me!

–Robert Browning Hamilton

6

STRETCH YOUR SOUL

REFUSE TO BE in a man-made environment day after day. You will run the grave risk of becoming dry, empty, and soulless like the materialism that surrounds you. There are at least two avenues of escape.

The first one is to give yourself to nature as often as you can. Go to the hills. Let the woods and rivers talk to you for a while and soften your soul. Have some of your business meetings and discussions in the park or on the beach, even at the risk of seeming strange. A lot more people will be doing it in the future. And besides, you will come up with more creative ideas.

Imagine rocks on the seashore. They just lie there, but from time to time the waves wash over and refresh them. Because of this, algae can grow around them and they are able to provide food for the fish. Like the rocks, if you want to be useful in any meaningful way, you must get wet from time to time. You must go into the woods and connect with nature to take charge.

Another way to stretch your soul is to decide to become a loving person. You don't even have to volunteer anywhere—just demonstrate a more sincere interest in every person you meet. Get in the habit of giving your love to people. Remember, love is a decision. Try to see the hurt and feel the pain in at least one person every day, and do something or say something nice in response. This is what love is; and love, the philosophers say, is the most powerful force in the world.

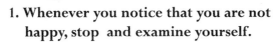

1. Whenever you notice that you are not happy, stop and examine yourself.

2. Recognize with heightened awareness where exactly you are and what you are doing.

3. Focus your awareness on your body and inside your body. Pay attention to your neck, chest, arms, legs, stomach, and back. Notice how these parts of your body feel. Simply notice. Remember that awareness leads to control.

4. If you can focus your awareness on a part of your body, you can change the feeling there.

Quick Prescription 6

- *Give yourself to nature as often as you can.*
- *Go into the woods and get charged to take charge.*
- *Decide to become a loving person: demonstrate a sincere interest in every person you meet.*

USE YOUR HAPPINESS AS A SHIELD AGAINST DISEASE

I have noticed that some patients are so deeply happy that they are able to exude happiness even in the presence of serious disease. Many of them seem to deliberately stir up their happiness as if to defy disease, and somehow they fare better.

I remember a 70-year-old woman who was diagnosed with terminal lung cancer. She came to the office every week and, despite the dismal prognosis, she was always very pleasant and jovial. She went out of her way to make the other patients laugh; you could always hear her in the waiting room, trying to cheer them up. She would often give up her turn to someone who was in a hurry, and she would tell a joke while she was being seen. She just did not know how to keep a smile off her face.

She lived much longer than expected.

This patient taught me that whatever predicament you're in, it is far healthier to develop a cheerful and happy attitude. This woman lived this philosophy and she, as well as many others, benefited from her courage to be happy in the face of disease.

7

CARRY POSITIVE BELIEFS WITH YOU WHEREVER YOU GO

WHAT YOU BELIEVE affects how happy you are. Beliefs have magic and power in them. If you go about your daily life without the advantage of positive beliefs, you are ignoring a ready source of great power and happiness. Positive beliefs give rise to positive feelings, and positive feelings can improve your performance in any field of endeavor. If you are not strong on beliefs, begin today to cultivate positive and relevant ones. Beliefs are like toothbrushes. You have to have at least one and you have to use it often, preferably several times a day. You can't use somebody else's. So get some beliefs and begin to use them to your advantage.

There are many categories of beliefs to consider. First, there is the belief in your own unique essence. This is a conviction that you have a specific purpose and that your life is significant and that you have a meaningful role to play in the world. This gives you confidence, and confidence and happiness go hand in hand.

The second category involves belief in God or a higher power or a mysterious life force outside of your self, or a belief that we are all connected to the whole universe in some unique way. This belief in your connection to the whole gives you a feeling of belonging and support, and a wider sense of significance.

The third category consists of everyday beliefs that influence your performance and your behavior in general. It is a good idea for you to make a list of the beliefs that affect your life in a positive way. If you carry a bundle of these positive beliefs with you wherever you go, and hold them at the forefront of your mind, they will influence your mood and enhance your achievements in a positive way.

QuickTips

Adopt some of these beliefs that can make your actions significant:
- everyone is capable of some great work in the world
- you can be happy in the midst of the storm
- good will prevail in the end
- where there is a will there is a way.

Please add some of your own to this short list. I suggest a bundle of 6 to 10 primary beliefs. They must be relevant and they must have enough energy to make a difference in the way you act.

Here are some more positive beliefs to put in your personal bundle:

- Every human being is worthy of my highest respect.
- I should never stand in the way of someone being himself or herself.
- My health is of paramount importance.
- Everything happens for a reason.
- Persistence is the opposite of failure.
- I have invincible powers within me.
- Honesty is the best policy.
- Whatever I set my mind to, I can achieve.

Look at your life. Examine the basic principles that govern your behavior, and see if you can come up with some beliefs that make sense for you. Write them down. Study them and let them become a part of your life, so that they can surface and influence your feelings and actions.

R

Quick Prescription 7

- *Begin today to cultivate positive and relevant beliefs.*
- *Believe in your unique essence.*
- *Believe we are all connected to the whole universe in some unique way.*
- *Make a list of the beliefs that affect your life in a positive way.*
- *Make your beliefs vibrant by thinking about them more often.*

Don't try to change the seasons,
the sunshine or the rain,

Don't try to change your neighbor,
'twill only bring you pain,

Use all that marvelous energy
that's bubbling in your head

To recognize your power and
change yourself instead.

8

BELIEVE THAT HAPPINESS
IS RELEVANT

EMBRACE THE BELIEF that the purpose of your life is to enjoy it. Believe that you are worthy of happiness. Believe that you are here to celebrate the universe. Believe that you are here to have a ball. Believe that happiness should permeate everything you do.

One reason so much unhappiness abounds is that we do not believe that happiness is relevant. We think that it is important to get on with life and be successful. This feeling that happiness is not really important as a permanent part of our lives makes it a stranger to us. When happiness surfaces to any significant degree, we question its authenticity and often force it to retreat out of sight, leaving us in our normal state of quiet desperation. We measure success in ways that have little to do with happiness; the idea of having happy feelings bubbling through us as we work, talk, or wait in line at the store is somehow a foreign concept. I would like you to believe that happiness is not only relevant, but it is key and must be a central part of everything you do.

I remember as a boy walking one day in the little village of Barbuda on my way to the family farm. I was passing by a beautiful beach not far from home. The sky was blue and the grass was green, the sun was shining brightly, and the birds were singing. The boats anchored in the harbor looked particularly colorful, and the muffled voices of the fishermen gave an aliveness to the whole atmosphere. I felt so happy as I walked along the beach that I began to skip and sing. At times when the road veered close to the beach, I would push my toes into the warm sand. I would sometimes stand still and, as the waves broke upon the beach, I would wait until the water almost touched my feet, and then I would suddenly run away.

After a while, it suddenly hit home that I was very happy. I noticed the feeling. I even enjoyed it for a second, and then I started to question it. "Why am I so happy today?" I asked myself. "Nothing has changed. I still have to walk several miles all alone in the blazing sun to find the garden while all the other boys are playing cricket in the schoolyard. Why am I so happy? I still have to face my father for the broken milk bottle. I have nothing to be happy about." And before I reached the iron gate that marked the end of the residential district, I was depressed again. The old familiar feelings of quiet discontent, faint anxiety, and gnawing dissatisfaction had settled, by my own invitation, deep in the center of my chest. In those days, I just could not accept the fact that happiness was part of my birthright. It was as if I were born to be good, to serve, or to help, and that it did not matter whether I was happy or not.

My advice is that you ensure your own happiness by deciding now to embrace the belief that happiness is relevant to you. Believe that you are on the planet to celebrate life, to enjoy every moment of your existence. Acknowledge deep down that you are worthy of happiness in your own right.

Write this:
- **Happiness is a big deal for me.**
- **The purpose of my life is to be happy, to enjoy every moment of my sojourn on this planet.**
- **The real purpose of life is to celebrate it.**

Write these words a second time but pretend that you are writing them indelibly on your brain. Then write them a third time, and this time, imagine that you are writing them on your heart.

Internalize the concept that happiness is central to your existence. Then, if you happen to wake up feeling happy for no apparent reason, you will nurture the feeling instead of frightening it away with foolish questions. All the while, you must be careful to recognize that happiness does not come from circumstances; it depends on you and what you decide to feel in whatever circumstances you may find yourself.

Isn't it amazing that something so powerful is entirely free and accessible to you at any time?

Quick Prescription 8

- *Believe that the purpose of your life is to enjoy it.*
- *Embrace the belief that happiness is relevant to your work.*
- *Acknowledge deep down that you are worthy of happiness in your own right.*
- *Internalize the concept that happiness is central to your existence.*
- *Recognize that happiness depends on you and what you decide to feel.*

In all the trade of war, no feat

Is nobler than a brave retreat.

–Samuel Butler

Sometimes it takes more strength to back down
than to move forward.

9

REMOVE STRESS
FROM YOUR RELATIONSHIPS

HAPPINESS DIES when it is not shared. Life is too precious to spend time nursing animosities and registering wrongs. Carry around a pocketful of forgiveness and sprinkle some of it in the face of anyone who hurts you.

QuickTips

If you are going to practice these techniques, you have to be a big person. You have to begin to see yourself as a strong person. You cannot be a weakling. Therefore, work hard on yourself to become more secure on the inside. You will need it. It's a hard road to travel but the rewards are unbeatable.

Here are some practical suggestions that can improve your relationships. Try to practice at least some of them until they become a habit.

1 Decide now that in any situation, negotiation, or confrontation that you are going to regard the human element as the most important variable. No matter what type of work you are doing, look

beyond the task, beyond the outcome. Take an exalted view of your function and grasp the opportunity to reach out and make a contribution. As Schopenhauer said, "People should be treated, not as a means to an end, but as an end in themselves."

2 Resolve that you will never allow the way that other people treat you to determine the way that you treat them. Always let your own values and principles determine how you will treat another person

3 Remember that about 90 percent of your joy in life will come from relationships; therefore, take time out every day to do or say something extra to deepen your relationships with others. Bring something new and different to people in your circle, and try to form and maintain happy and interesting relationships in which you can express your true self and have others do the same.

4 Try to make people feel good about themselves. Any contact with another human being can have one of three outcomes: the person can go away feeling worse, they can go away feeling the same, or they can go away feeling better. Make sure that people go away feeling much better about themselves after speaking to you. This will help you feel better about yourself.

5 Make it your way of life to back away from unpleasant, confrontational encounters. Don't fight unless you have to. Remember that in all the trade of war, no feat is nobler than a brave retreat. Learn to sacrifice being right in favor of being happy.

6 Know your "walk away" position. Know what is too much for you to take. Know how far you will let things slide before you put your foot down. Think about your values and principles and allow them to guide you in your interactions with others. Let them determine how far you allow yourself to go in any situation.

7 Be sincere in all you say and do. Remember that human beings have the uncanny ability to detect insincerity.

8 Look for the good in others and compliment them. Kenneth Blanchard, co-author of *The One Minute Manager*, suggests, "Try and catch people doing something right or even approximately right," and compliment them for it. Refrain from criticism. It leads to unhappy feelings, and what goes around comes around.

9 Listen more than you talk.

10 Overlook mistakes more often. When your partner behaves like a jerk, overlook it sometimes, but not every time. When your child makes a mistake, overlook it sometimes, unless it is serious. If your boss snaps at you, shrug it off this once. Don't feel the need to respond to every insult. Learn to throw a hunk of silence at some criticisms and encourage peace. Happiness thrives in an atmosphere of peace.

11 Learn to suspend your natural resentment in any confrontation and to consider the viewpoint of the aggressor. You can usually disarm the aggressor by jumping to his side.

12 Actively seek positive emotions: joy, peace, love, confidence, and hope. Embrace these feelings and express them in your daily contacts with others. Spend some time thinking about them and reading about them so that they become an integral part of your life.

13 Filter out negative emotions. Put a membrane around yourself so that only positive, useful, nurturing emotions will filter through from the environment. When you encounter someone who is abrasive and rude, you will not take in any negative feelings such as hostility, anger, hatred, or resentment. They will be filtered out, leaving you with the positive feelings previously mentioned. In this way, you will respond to negative behavior with positive words and actions, and you will overcome evil with good.

14 Be careful not to imbibe the negative feelings and then suppress them. This is not healthy. You must make a decision before the fact that you are going to use hardships, difficulties, insults, put downs, and the like to strengthen your psycho-physiological system. Einstein said that in every difficulty there is opportunity, so program yourself to meet these emotions when they are thrown at you, with the singular determination to use them as cues to create a refined and integrated body and mind. They do not have to exert any power over you.

15 Work hard on yourself with these exercises and your happiness will soar.

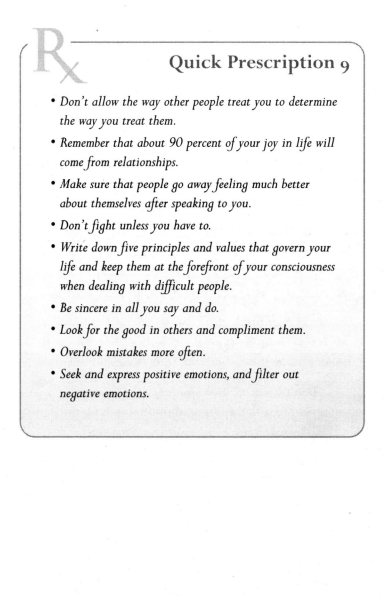

Quick Prescription 9

- *Don't allow the way other people treat you to determine the way you treat them.*
- *Remember that about 90 percent of your joy in life will come from relationships.*
- *Make sure that people go away feeling much better about themselves after speaking to you.*
- *Don't fight unless you have to.*
- *Write down five principles and values that govern your life and keep them at the forefront of your consciousness when dealing with difficult people.*
- *Be sincere in all you say and do.*
- *Look for the good in others and compliment them.*
- *Overlook mistakes more often.*
- *Seek and express positive emotions, and filter out negative emotions.*

DON'T BE A J.E.R.K.

A **J.E.R.K.** is a person who is always judging others, who is egotistical and rapped up in himself or herself, who is always too rigid to change, who is always criticizing other people and who is knotted up inside and carries this tension into all relationships.

Don't Judge People. If someone is different, don't judge him or her. If they act differently, be curious and find out more. Learn to explore the unfamiliar without the limitation of a judgmental attitude. Be quick to praise and slow to criticize. Judgment and criticism go hand in hand.

Don't Be Egotistical. Don't deliberately boost your ego, especially if it makes others look less worthy. Boost the egos of others instead. A jerk is a self-centered person who thinks that other people are on the planet just to serve, honor, and praise him or her.

Beware of Rigidity. Rigidity leads to collapse. Learn to be flexible. Learn to bend. Sometimes it is in backing down that you discover the true meaning of integrity. Learn to surrender sometimes.

Don't Criticize. Find something to praise instead. A jerk is slow to compliment others and quick to blame. Relinquish blame, and praise whenever possible.

Avoid the "knots" in relationships. Be a tension tamer and not a tension builder. Try to relax and remove the knots of tension from your own body and then seek to ease the tension in your relationships at home and among your friends and colleagues. One way to avoid knots is to spot conflicts before they begin and back away from them.

10

RAISE YOUR EMOTIONAL IQ

EMOTIONS DETERMINE SO MUCH about our lives and yet we are not aware of them and their subtle yet powerful influence unless they loom too large or perhaps linger too long. We are busy doing our work and emotions are busy doing their work in us and it isn't until someone says something that we realize how miserable or how bitter we are really feeling.

This book is designed to help us enjoy our short journey through life, and to do that, we have to wake up and own our emotions, recognize them for what they are, and really learn how to master them. How we do that will determine the degree to which we can make ourselves happy.

QuickTips

Most stressors are emotional. The way you feel about someone or something in your life can trigger stress hormones that can have devastating effects on your heart and your immune system, whether you are aware of it or not. This is a good time to decide to become a master of your emotions.

Here are five things you can do to raise your emotional IQ:

1 Become more aware of your emotions. Emotions are impulses of energy that are an immediate summation of our experiences, both mentally and physically. Your emotions gauge how your past and present experiences are affecting your physiology at any moment. You have to take time to notice this, and, as you do, you will gain control over the way you feel. And control leads to happiness. Notice what you are feeling and how you are feeling at any given point in your day. Right now, put your attention on different parts of your body. First notice your head, then your neck, your chest, your stomach, your legs, and finally, your feet. Try to identify the quality and intensity of sensation that is lurking around in each part.

2 Learn specific ways to understand and control your emotions. Emotions have two components: the basic feeling tone that dominates your consciousness at any given time, the feelings you tend to have unrelated to what is going on and the feelings that come as a result of your immediate reactions to events and situations. To be a happier person, you must refuse to let events and circumstances determine the quality of the feelings that flow through your body and mind. Do not react to events with negative feelings. If someone calls you a fool, don't let ugly, vengeful feelings fill your soul on account of their poor judgment. You can either block these feelings from entering your physiology with the power of your thoughts, attitude, intention, and actions, or choose to nurture them.

Whenever you encounter an unpleasant situation, it would be far better to smile, assume a relaxed posture, and intend to be happy. Take a deep, slow, breath and feel the wonderful flow of oxygen permeating your system. At the same time, use the memory of some pleasant experience to trigger the flow of positive feelings. Do whatever you have to do to feel good. Respond to the difficulties of life in a way that is self-enhancing and good for the soul.

3   Focus on becoming self-motivated. Don't be controlled or motivated by what others would do or say, or how they may regard you
in the light of your achievements. Do the things that will make
your life significant. Let your motivation surface from within.
Write down your goals—the things you want to do. Make sure
that they conform to your inner sense of purpose. In this way, your
conduct will be motivated by what your life is about, and your
level of motivation will not be at the mercy of what comes or goes.

4   Adopt an optimistic attitude in every situation. Recognize the piv-
otal importance and power of hope and don't leave home without
it. Decide now—right now, even as you are reading this—that you
are going to be optimistic in all your encounters and especially
when things go wrong. When your parents say you are a big disap-
pointment to them, hope. When your boss yells at you for getting
it wrong, hope. When your lover runs off with someone else,
hope. Hope is a verb. It is something you do. Program hope and
optimism into your life. Intend to always look on the bright side of
any situation. Tell yourself that if you are going to be happy in life,
you simply cannot afford one more pessimistic thought. To adopt a
pessimistic attitude in response to any situation is to set yourself up
for defeat. Imagine a positive outcome and behave as if it were
inevitable. Be an eternal optimist. This is how you build a happy
future—not from your past, not from your fears, not from your
circumstances, but from your sense of hope. Aren't you glad that
hope is a decision?

5   Get along with others. Andrew Carnegie underlined the importance of this social skill when he agreed to pay his employees more
for the ability to get along with people than for any other single
skill.

Jean Paul Sartre said that hell is other people and I am sure you feel
that way sometimes. The real secret in getting along with others is
to recognize the great gulf of differences between you and any
other human being and to approach everyone with curiosity and to
banish judgment. Every human being has a unique load of feelings,

needs, beliefs, and desires and we will be successful in dealing with each person if we can decipher what he or she is carrying and respond to it appropriately. This is the master skill of getting along with others and it is called listening.

Many of my patients have undertaken to practice these five techniques and have reported greater happiness as a result. I hope you will find at least one or two if not all five useful. I am sure you know them already. But knowing them is not enough. Practice them and you will become a happier person.

Quick Prescription 10

- *Become more aware of your emotions.*
- *Be able to verbalize what you are feeling at any given time.*
- *Let the difficulties you encounter inspire you to become a happier person.*
- *Know your purpose and let your motivation surface from within.*
- *Adopt an optimistic attitude in every situation.*
- *Imagine a positive outcome and behave as if it were inevitable.*
- *In dealing with others, banish judgment and embrace curiosity.*

Alas! By some degree of woe,

We every bliss, must gain:

The heart can ne'er a transport know,

That never feels a pain

–Lord Lyttleton

11

GAIN POWER OVER EMOTIONS

MANY OF MY PATIENTS REPORT that they have great difficulty getting rid of negative emotions. They say that feelings of guilt, anger, worry, sadness, or anxiety flood their minds and they feel powerless to stop them.

I have developed a little formula for conquering negative emotions. It has been very effective in my medical practice and I would like to pass it on to you.

If fear is trying to capture your attention, focus on love.

QuickTips

Remember that emotions have no power of their own. You have to feed them with your thoughts, your energy, and your intention. They are like visitors to your home who hang around too long and wear you out. This is how you get rid of these visitors: ignore them and pay attention to the positive opposite.

1 **Set an emotion-detection alarm.** Get in the habit of checking your feelings as often as you can, and identifying the predominant

emotion that you are experiencing at any given moment. Try it now. What emotions are you experiencing right now? When the emotion is negative, your alarm will go off and you will be in a position to change your feelings.

2 **Carry a bundle of positive beliefs with you wherever you go.** Live with powerful beliefs. Include among them the belief that you can master your emotions.

3 **Create a chest of memories of positive events that you have experienced.** Memories can trigger positive emotions. Choose an experience from your past that was predominantly joyful. Embellish and recall it often in your imagination. Make the situation big, bright, and colorful. If it was a banquet, try to recall the smell and the taste of the food and try to hear the sound of dishes and happy people talking and laughing. Get all your five senses involved whenever you create the scene. Think about this scene often. Let it occupy a special place in your mind, and when sad feelings threaten to predominate, go to this special place in your mind, open this chest of memories, and the feelings associated with the memories will flow through your body and mind.

Create a chest of memories for the different emotions that you want to be able to summon at will. Include memories of a joyful occasion to use when you feel sad, and memories of a time when you were experiencing high-level energy to use when you feel lethargic. In these stressful times, you also need to put away memories of relaxing times on a beach or in a beautiful park. You need to open this chest of memories when you are feeling tense, and the original feelings of relaxation will come over you once again. Do not forget to create a chest of loving memories to replace feelings of hostility and anger. It is amazing that simply by using your imagination to create and recall a desired situation, you can completely change your emotions.

4 **Change your internal dialogue.** If you feel unhappy and hateful whenever you have to talk to your boss, listen first to what you are saying to yourself and change the conversation. Tell yourself that this is an opportunity to shine. You can even say, "I love to talk to my boss," as you think of possible outcomes and opportunities that can ensue from the contact. Changing your internal conversation will change your feeling, but speak convincingly and sincerely to yourself.

5 **Visualize yourself handling a difficult situation masterfully.** See this happening over and over in your mind's eye and this will change your emotions. You will feel more in control.

6 **Keep your mind on what you want.** Keep it off what you don't want.

Quick Prescription 11

- *Set an emotion-detection alarm to identify negative feelings as soon as they emerge.*
- *Carry the positive belief that you can master your emotions.*
- *Create a chest of memories of positive events to trigger positive emotions.*
- *Change your internal dialogue to change your feelings.*
- *Speak convincingly and sincerely to yourself.*
- *Visualize yourself in a challenging situation, handling it masterfully.*
- *Keep your mind on what you want out of every activity and keep it off what you don't want.*

You carry your happiness with you into
the morning or into the twilight;
don't expect to find it along the way.

Happiness is where you are!

12

ASK YOURSELF, "WHAT'S SO BAD ABOUT FEELING DEPRESSED?"

ONE OF THE MISTAKES WE MAKE in this society is that we do not tarry long enough in our predicaments to get anything of value from them. When we are feeling depressed, we are in such a hurry to feel good again that we miss the message that depression might be trying to convey. We lack the patience or the inclination to wade through the rubble to see what we can uncover about ourselves. Depression reveals to us invaluable secrets that would otherwise remain hidden. It can be a tremendous springboard to a better life.

Trouble struck my family recently. I was depressed, annoyed, and anxious. Instead of running immediately to a doctor for a prescription to find a ready way out of the cloud of negative feelings, I looked at my symptoms as a gift. I regarded them as teachers to show me what I otherwise could not see. In a sense, I welcomed my depression. I made friends with it. I used it as a window from which I could look at the world and at myself from a new perspective, and that gave me great vision and strength. When the problems disappeared and the thick clouds of inertia and sadness lifted, I was almost sorry to see something so valuable to me disappear from my life. It was like saying goodbye to a friend from another city who had come to visit. His presence may have imposed some restrictions and painful inconveniences, but oh, the wealth of wisdom that accrued to me!

To a great extent I think we should regard our periods of depression in this way. Not that we should hang on to them forever, but we should recognize that they come with gifts. They have something to offer, and we want to be intimate enough with them, and spend enough time with them, to seize the prize that they offer.

Thomas Moore, author of *Care of the Soul*, talks about the saturnine qualities of depression in a very inspiring way. He almost makes you want your next bout of sadness to strike so that you will do the necessary dissection to find the gift that accompanies it. He talks about the obvious cycles of life. Sometimes we are lifted up and sometimes we are weighted down. When we are down, we take on the qualities of Saturn. We become "saturnized." The experience of being saturnized has many dimensions to it. When we are depressed, we often feel drained, lethargic, and weary. So we pull the blinds and go to bed. And it is through our window while we are in bed that we may see a view of the city or of ourselves that would otherwise elude us.

Beware of fast cures. Furthermore, beware of being so focused on the cure, or the way you want to feel, that you miss the experience of the depression and what it has to say to you.

One of the unpleasant emotions that accompany depression is a feeling of detachment—"a faraway feeling," as one of my patients usually describes it. This faraway feeling is akin to being on Saturn, which is one of the planets farthest from the sun. Detachment and emotional distance are often a part of this experience; perhaps if you are in this place you can lean into the "Saturnine experience" and see what happens. Maybe, when the clouds lift, you will have a new angle on intimacy and you may be able to value and manage emotional distance or emotional closeness more appropriately.

What's my point in all this? Am I saying that you should go out and get depressed? Not at all! Am I saying that my patients should throw away the medications that I myself prescribe for depression? Of course not! All I am saying is that you should give your symptoms a chance to help you navigate your way to greater happiness. Don't run away from them. Work through them. This will give you inner strength, and inner strength is the foundation of real happiness.

What about people who are stuck in a deep depression and can't get out? Such people are often so frightened by their feelings and by their predicament that they are focused on knocking down the walls and escaping from the experience. They are not living the moment. Perhaps it is too frightening. They are obsessed with wishing their way out of the horrible experience without actually taking the time to acknowledge what it really has to offer. But if they would just stop, tarry, and listen for a while, avenues of escape or improvement that had earlier seemed out of their reach would suddenly and miraculously appear. This is where a good therapist can help.

QuickTips

Research has demonstrated that the brain deteriorates if depression goes untreated. Therefore, don't be reluctant to get help if you have the diagnosis of depression. It's okay to take a pill if it's appropriate. But also accept the challenge to get involved and do as much as possible to help yourself.

Don't be terrified by your depression. Accept it. Face it. Identify it, and notice the pain. This is an enriching way to go through the dark periods of your life. Get some professional support while you try to learn from your sadness. Don't waste your pain. Make it count to improve your life.

The good thing about all this is that you can milk your symptoms for their value, even if you are in therapy. You can gain this kind of insight and advantage even when an antidepressant drug is working its miracle on you. The trick is not to abdicate responsibility but to face your symptoms, suck strength from them, and soar like an eagle to new heights of happiness and joy.

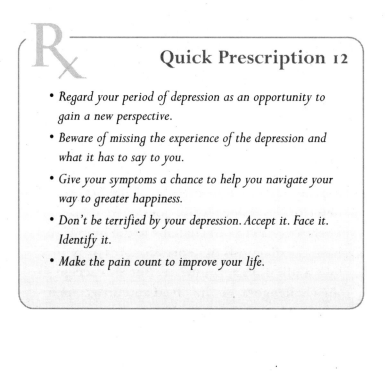

Quick Prescription 12

- *Regard your period of depression as an opportunity to gain a new perspective.*
- *Beware of missing the experience of the depression and what it has to say to you.*
- *Give your symptoms a chance to help you navigate your way to greater happiness.*
- *Don't be terrified by your depression. Accept it. Face it. Identify it.*
- *Make the pain count to improve your life.*

He that strides across the highest mountains
laughs at all tragedies.

–Nietzsche

13

FOSTER A CAN-DO ATTITUDE

BEWARE OF THE INNER VOICE THAT WHISPERS, "I can't." Self-doubt is a major stumbling block on the road to happiness. In stress research the issue of perception is very big. If you have to face a difficulty and you perceive that you can handle it, you suffer almost no stress from it, whereas if you perceive that it is outside of your control and there is nothing you can do about it, you open the floodgates of stress with all its attendant problems. This is why it is crucial for you to learn to boost your perception and foster a can-do attitude.

QuickTips

Thinking you're not in control opens the gate wide to stress. When faced with a stressor, always assume a challenge response and tell yourself, *"I can handle it."* Let these four words be a constant part of your daily vocabulary.

Here's how to foster a can-do attitude and develop feelings of confidence:

1   When faced with a daunting task, be extra clear about what you want to achieve. Re-examine and redefine your goal. Write down your goal and review it until it is abundantly clear to you and can

be articulated in a concise and meaningful fashion to anyone. Fifty percent of what you achieve will be derived from just being certain of the objective.

2   Focus on your strengths. Acknowledge your special talents and innate gifts. Reflect on which of your special skills will be required for this particular project. Is it your ability to communicate? Is it your facility with figures? Is it your artistic insight? Always try to match your level and quality of skill with the demands of the task.

3   Heighten the feelings of joy and excitement that you experience as you initiate the project. You can do this by expecting that good things will happen to you as you embark on the project. Use your power of expectation. Happy, optimistic music can also stimulate positive feelings in your mind.

4   Adjust your posture to match that of a very happy and confident person. Smile, laugh, hold your shoulders back without tension, and think the thoughts that are consistent with a joyful physiology. Do this often during your day.

5   Watch how you use your energy supply. Remember that your energy is limited. Focus your energy like a laser beam upon the task at hand and, whenever possible, remember to take time out to recover from the strain of your activity. Internalize the word recovery. It is very important. After you have worked hard for a while, take a break and make sure your body and brain recover from the stress that might have been building up.

As you recover, take time to bank your energy by consciously breathing deeply and easily, by relaxing your muscles, and by letting go of any negative thoughts. Just stop doing. Surrender. Sometimes our frantic efforts get in the way, and the best avenue of progress is to do nothing for a while and listen to the inner prompting of the soul. Get recharged. Let your mind go blank and concentrate on a sense of deep inner peace. In this way you will cultivate an invaluable feeling of quiet physical abundance and inner readiness for action.

6   One simple action is to breathe slowly and evenly, and extend the out-breath for as long as possible. This will relax your muscles and make more energy available to the brain. In addition to these measures, maintain a relaxed posture: let your neck and jaw be loose and your back become long and wide.

7   Make sure that your beliefs are consistent with what you want to achieve. Remember to introduce some self-enhancing beliefs about what you are doing. Believe, for example, that you will be a smashing success and relinquish any doubts that restrain you.

   Your capacity to believe is an awesome force. Believe that you are capable. Believe that you will be articulate and bright in any encounter. Positive beliefs will definitely affect the outcome of any undertaking. Beliefs have magic and power in them, and yet they are free to all. You will notice that believing is a recurring theme in this book.

8   Love what you do, and love the people involved. Love, just like happiness, is a decision. As mentioned elsewhere, you can jump-start the process of putting love in your heart by acting as if it were already there.

   Love conserves energy and motivates others to move on your behalf. Besides, love makes you want to give, and since it is far better to give than to receive, you develop a good feeling about yourself and the way you live your life. And when you feel good, your performance soars.

9   Intensify the focus of your attention. Look for the joy, the mystery, and the fun in every aspect of your work. Joy is in the details. Look diligently for it.

10 Begin to feel that you can make a success of whatever is before you. Think that you can, tell yourself that you can, and imagine an enjoyable process and positive outcome. Then act with the confidence that you can produce the results that you want.

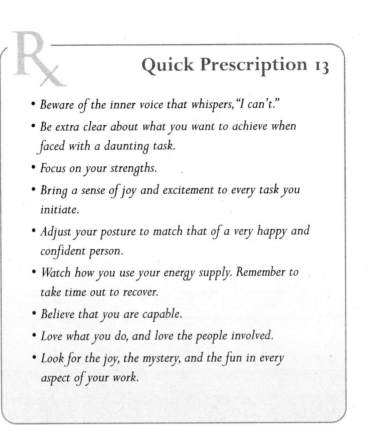

Quick Prescription 13

- *Beware of the inner voice that whispers, "I can't."*
- *Be extra clear about what you want to achieve when faced with a daunting task.*
- *Focus on your strengths.*
- *Bring a sense of joy and excitement to every task you initiate.*
- *Adjust your posture to match that of a very happy and confident person.*
- *Watch how you use your energy supply. Remember to take time out to recover.*
- *Believe that you are capable.*
- *Love what you do, and love the people involved.*
- *Look for the joy, the mystery, and the fun in every aspect of your work.*

Paradise is where I am.

—Voltaire

14

COMPARTMENTALIZE

MY FAMILY AND I SPENT FIVE DAYS in the beautiful Austrian town of Schladming in the heart of summer. The mountains sparkled in the sunshine, the birds sang, and pretty, multicolored wildflowers decorated the windowsills of all the houses in the region. The church bell pealed a beautiful reminder that time was of the essence. The shopkeepers, dressed in local green-and-gold outfits, enthusiastically recounted the history of their town to visitors in search of information. A beautiful river meandered and gurgled through the middle of town, lending its greenish blue tint to blend with the bright colors of the surrounding houses and stores.

People walked leisurely through the little town, stopping occasionally to admire the picturesque landscape; little old ladies on green bicycles jostled with cars and made their way to the bakery. You couldn't paint a more idyllic scene in your imagination. It was an enchanting and uplifting experience. At least so I was told—I was there but missed it all.

Even though I was present in body, my mind was miles away. I was preoccupied with an impending misfortune where I grew up. A hurricane had just destroyed parts of Florida and was heading towards my hometown. That is where I really was. My body was in Schladming but my mind was in the valley of despair, worrying about what might go wrong. And so I missed the whole experience.

For years after, I heard my family members describe the days in Schladming. They laughed about something that happened in a little shop on the way to the chairlift. They often referred to the way the houses were decorated. They were in awe of the experience. I could not remember a thing; I just was not there.

It was after this trip that I decided I was going to always live in the present and not allow what is pending for tomorrow to prevent me from enjoying today. I trained my mind. I worked hard on living in the present. I was deliberate and relentless. I remember repeating to myself several times a day, "Wherever you are, be there."

A few years after my visit to Schladming, I was going to St. Lucia with my family to stay in a beautiful villa a few feet from the beach. It was an ideal Caribbean spot and the house had its own beach, on a bay calm and unruffled like a large swimming pool. I was looking forward to this holiday with great anticipation. My patients could sense my happiness and commented on it.

Just as I was about to leave for the airport, a man arrived and asked me my name. I proudly identified myself and he handed me an official-looking document. It was a summons to appear in court. A patient was suing my clinic for several thousand dollars—and I was about to depart for one of the best vacations I had ever planned.

In an effort not to repeat the Schladming experience, I realized that I could not do anything about this matter for several months. It was very serious but not particularly urgent. I could wait until I returned to respond. Going to court is always a serious matter, but I was determined to put this problem in a special compartment and lock it away until the appropriate time after my vacation. I told no one about it. I simply focused on having a great time. The flight was delightful. My kids were as high as kites in the sky, their eyes scintillating with joy. I allowed myself to feel a profound happiness, which I did not let the memory of my troubles extinguish.

Many times during the vacation, while swimming, climbing, or sitting on a rock watching the waves, my mind would drift to my court appearance; however, I quickly refocused on the present and savored everything I could about it.

After two weeks I returned home from the best vacation I had ever had. And I was there every minute of every day. I learned to compartmentalize, and that is how I managed to remain happy, even though something unpleasant was hovering over my future.

As it happened, when I returned to my office I learned that the whole thing had been dropped, and all my worries would have been in vain.

Since then I have learned that if I have to face an unpleasant audience on a Monday morning, I can still have a great weekend. If I have to go to the doctor to check a lump I notice in my breast (and men do get breast cancer), I can still enjoy myself until I have to deal with that reality.

Truth be told, there will always be something hanging over us that could prevent us from enjoying the present moment. We must resolve to enjoy today, even if we are going to the hospital for a biopsy tomorrow. We must learn to live with gusto, even though we are certain that we are going to die. This is the story of the human race. We all know that the shadow of death is hanging over us. We live with the constant reminder that we are all going to die. Should we allow this to stop us from enjoying the time we do have?

The ability to compartmentalize—suspend our anxieties, lock away our troubles, and enjoy the moment—is an important skill in the pursuit of a happy life. In order to acquire this skill, begin with small challenges. Use the everyday experiences of your life to practice the discipline of compartmentalizing.

If your 17-year-old daughter is going on a date with a man you don't know very well and, as soon as they drive off, your happiness evaporates and a host of "what ifs" invade your mind, begin right there and then to practice compartmentalizing. Don't give yourself time to think unwarranted thoughts, and if you do and they get out of hand, tell yourself, "I'd better be more positive." Right at the beginning say, "I am going to be happy until nine o'clock, and after that I will deal with the situation." Having made the decision, suspend your reaction and focus on enjoying your life in the meantime.

If you are waiting for your wife to come home from work and foolish worries pop into your head, don't stand by the window and pace up and down, letting anxiety swell. Instead, tell yourself you will remain happy until seven or eight o'clock, and then you will worry, if you feel you must. The trick is to give worry as little time as possible.

When I started my practice, I used to worry my head off if no one showed up for a while and the waiting room stayed empty. I would think about the rent, the insurance, and the other mounting expenses and wonder how I was going to make it if no one came to my clinic. I would even think to myself, "What kind of doctor has an empty waiting room?"

I soon learned to make the decision not to worry for thirty minutes. That gave me thirty minutes of internal peace. I would set out to do something useful such as reading an article about hepatitis C. I made a conscious decision that I was going to be happy during this time. Usually before the time was up I would be busy again, and I would not have been degraded by worry and the other negative emotions that usually accompany it.

QuickTips

Sufficient unto the day is the evil there of. Take no thought for tomorrow for tomorrow will think for itself.
—Matthew 6:34

So to increase the happiness in your life, use this simple trick when difficulties arise. Tell yourself that you will forget about the problem for now, but that you will pick it up in five minutes, or one hour, or one day, or one year. Meanwhile, make a firm decision that you are going to focus your energies on doing what you have to do, and squeeze as much joy as you can out of every moment of life.

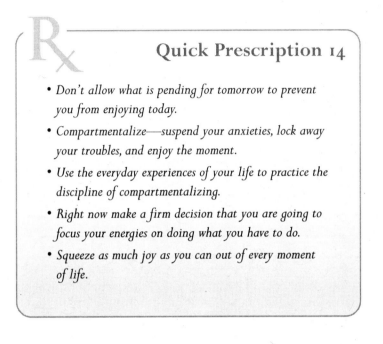

Quick Prescription 14

- *Don't allow what is pending for tomorrow to prevent you from enjoying today.*
- *Compartmentalize—suspend your anxieties, lock away your troubles, and enjoy the moment.*
- *Use the everyday experiences of your life to practice the discipline of compartmentalizing.*
- *Right now make a firm decision that you are going to focus your energies on doing what you have to do.*
- *Squeeze as much joy as you can out of every moment of life.*

For any conscious being to live is to change, to change is to grow, and to grow is to go on creating oneself anew endlessly.

–Bergson

15

RECOGNIZE THAT
HAPPINESS IS GROWTH

MANY YEARS AGO I was sitting at an airport in the Caribbean. Six teenaged students who were flying off to university had just arrived at the counter. One of them had to return to the curb to collect his hand luggage and as he passed close to the bench on which I was seated, I noticed the Latin words *"Qui non proficit, deficit"* printed on his blazer. For years I tried to figure out the meaning of those words. They have become a permanent part of my memory. It was not until three years later that I learned their true meaning: "He who doesn't move forward is moving backward."

This underlines the fact that life and the ability to move are as one. If at the end of today you are no better, or no happier, or no wiser, you are not as you were yesterday—you are worse. If you are not moving forward, you are moving backward. If you do not grow, you are out of synchrony with life.

Henry Bergson, a nineteenth-century French philosopher, said, "For a conscious being, to exist is to change, to change is to mature, to mature is to go on creating oneself anew endlessly." Adler, the great psychiatrist, remarked that it was wonderful that we could continue to grow and change ourselves and become better and better for as long as we live. And this innate excitement of renewal and change is what I think happiness is. Happiness is growth. We are happy when we are growing—growing in knowledge, growing in patience, growing in love, growing out of a divorce, growing out of despair into the arena of hope. "Oh, what a wonderful life this is! I only wish I had realized it sooner."

QuickTips

Be always working on some aspect of yourself. Create your own university and elevate your life intellectually, emotionally, and spiritually.

Here are some guidelines to help you ensure you are moving in the right direction:

- Stop seeing yourself as a frozen and fixed entity. See yourself not as you are, but as you are becoming. Think of yourself as a center of change.

- Next, become the architect of your own ultimate potential. Do something every day to build happiness in your life. Work daily to improve different aspects of your life. Work hard on improving yourself, your disposition, your emotional fortitude, your discipline, and your health. Work harder on yourself than you do on your job.

- Build a routine whereby you go into solitude every day, even for five minutes. The advice to seek out silence and solitude is repeated several times in this book in the hope that it will become second nature to you to spend time alone in silence. Refer to the guidelines in Chapter 2, Ask Yourself, "Who Am I and What Am I Doing Here?"

- Read a book every month that can help you develop a particular area of your life. You can create a book club for this purpose and meet with friends to discuss ideas from your readings.

- Buy audiotapes or CDs and listen to them in your car or while exercising. To save money, buy these tapes or CDs with friends and circulate them. Spend your money on developing yourself and you will make it back by leaps and bounds.

- Create a mastermind alliance group—four people who will meet for one hour every two weeks or so to discuss personal progress in the areas of health, family, finance, career, and spiritual development.

If you take steps like these to advance your knowledge, increase your wisdom, and grow positive qualities, you will become a happier and more fulfilled individual. The more you learn, the more you stimulate the brain, and the happier you will be. And the more time you spend reflecting on your knowledge and experience, the wiser you will become.

Repeat this sentence over and over again: "Happiness is growth." If someone asks you what aspect of your work you are concentrating on, you would probably be able to answer without any hesitation. Likewise, you should be able to answer just as readily if someone asks you what aspect of your personality or yourself you are working on.

R̲x̲ Quick Prescription 15

- *Endeavor to be better, happier, and wiser than you were yesterday.*
- *See yourself not as you are, but as you are becoming.*
- *Become the architect of your own potential.*
- *Work harder on yourself than you do on your job.*
- *Take steps to advance your knowledge, increase your wisdom, and grow positive qualities.*
- *Repeat over and over again, "Happiness is growth."*

Concentrate not on the elimination of the undesired condition, but rather on the creation of the condition desired.

–Olga Worrell

16

EXPERIENCE THE
ENCHANTED WORLD

WE LIVE IN AN ENCHANTED WORLD full of meaning, mysteries, and fun. But for so many of us, money, jobs, and difficult relationships predominate. We must be relentless in our determination to experience the enchanted world or we will become trapped in the clutches of materiality.

Although I am in the middle of a busy career, I try to develop what the poet Rilke calls "an infinite muscle of reception." This is an attitude of mind that compels me to stay open to experiencing the simple mysteries of everyday life. I often try to do as Blake's poem suggests: "See the world in a grain of sand, and beauty in a wildflower." This is the kind of awareness that I often ask my patients to develop—a heliotropic awareness, where you are like the plant that is forever turning towards the light. We too must be intent on turning towards the light and finding the meaning in all things.

This openness to the mystery of the world invites epiphanies into our lives—those rare moments of sudden awakening that are intensely pleasurable and enlightening. Epiphanies have the amazing capacity to transform our psychophysiological state. They make us happy in a very profound way.

I remember once looking out the window and seeing a bird ravenously going after some cherries and then returning to its young in a nest in another tree. As I witnessed this rather commonplace occurrence, for some reason I felt high and lifted up. I had an epiphany. Another time I was on the upper level of my house, and I heard my children laughing together in another room. And there was that inexplicable feeling of joy again! These feelings are invaluable gifts that I receive from time to time, and they enrich my day.

The only problem is that epiphanies are usually rare. However, if you constantly seek after the positive and the mysterious, your life will be more in tune with the inexplicable joys of nature, and epiphanies will appear more often.

QuickTips

Try to hold your next meeting in a nature setting instead of in a restaurant or an office. Sit under a tree to talk business and stretch your soul even as you discuss work. Let the inspiraton from nature dilute the drudgery of work.

Here are a few practical ideas to help you develop your muscle of infinite reception and bring the enchanted world and more epiphanies into your life:

- Think of the world as a happy place, full of mysteries and unseen pleasures to be explored and enjoyed. Do that even if you are driving home in a city full of concrete buildings.

- Do the ordinary, mundane tasks in an extraordinary way. Bring a sense of joy and wonder and elegance to everything you do. Ask yourself, "What's my style?" and bring your personal style in all its uniqueness to the ordinary events of your life. Do it with flair.

- Focus on the present moment. Give it all you have. When talking to your daughter, for example, talk with your whole heart and listen with your soul. Look for the joy and the mystery in what you might otherwise think is another ordinary conversation. See what you see and hear what you hear.

- Listen to the songs of life. Hear the breeze in the trees, the waves kissing the rocks, the rain touching the earth, or the water hugging the sand. Listen and you will hear what others cannot hear because they do not tune their ears to the divine sounds that echo in the universe.

- Don't forget to dance. Dance every morning as you realize that the gift of life and the pleasures of nature are renewed every day. Dance as you notice the grass rising up above the earth. Dance as you see the mountains high and lifted up towards the heavens.

- Give yourself permission to be easily impressed with the wonders in the universe. See greatness everywhere and wonder at it. Recognize that not everything is subject to our narrow understanding of life. Nature is bigger and broader and vaster than we can ever know. Leave room in your life and your intellect to appreciate it all.

- Look for an uplifting, exuberant feeling just from being alive. Look diligently and you will find it.

- Look for points of joy in troublesome circumstances. Look for beauty in the storm.

- Develop a soulful relationship to everything. Look beyond function. Look for the mystery. Look at your computer and listen to the silent story of mystery and feel the connection that goes beyond what it can do for you.

- Don't neglect your exercise routine. Exercise can jump-start the process of happiness and give you a feeling of exhilaration and exuberance.

- Be more impressed with the little miracles of your life, such as your ability to hear, or walk, or feel.

- Punctuate your day with meaningful pauses just to appreciate who you are and all the benefits of life that you enjoy.

- Embrace the fact that you are wonderfully and fearfully made. Be amazed that in all the world there is no one else like you. You are unique.

- In everything, give thanks.

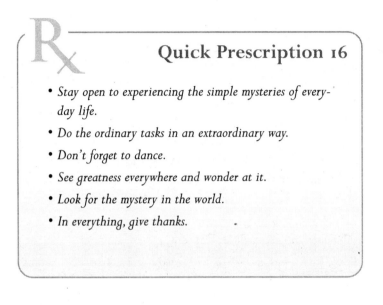

Quick Prescription 16

- *Stay open to experiencing the simple mysteries of everyday life.*
- *Do the ordinary tasks in an extraordinary way.*
- *Don't forget to dance.*
- *See greatness everywhere and wonder at it.*
- *Look for the mystery in the world.*
- *In everything, give thanks.*

If you want happiness for an hour—take a nap.

If you want happiness for a day—go fishing.

If you want happiness for a month—get married.

If you want happiness for a year—inherit a fortune.

If you want happiness for a lifetime—help others.

–Chinese Proverb

17

BEWARE OF SPEED

EVERYONE I KNOW IS IN A HURRY. We have moved "from a world where the big eat the small to one where the fast eat the slow." We are convinced that if we are going to amount to anything we must hurry. Speed is a sign of success in most circles. And this is how we live our lives, hurrying from one engagement to another, rushing from one job to the next, ignoring the very instrument that makes it all possible. It is as if some authority figure is constantly whispering in our ears, "Hurry up." We have developed a chronic sense of urgency and it has penetrated the fabric of our lives. This addiction to speed is a cause of great unhappiness. We have no time for ourselves, no time to nurture our inner life, and happiness dwindles away. An amazing 80 percent of what we are busy doing is of no consequence.

The fact is that speed is an impostor and time is an illusion. If you are able to get your mind around this concept, you will begin to be a happier person.

Time is no more than a way of measuring our activities. If we are completely captivated by the process of measurement, then the activity itself suffers from a woeful lack of attention, and speed ends up robbing us of the supreme thrill of achievement. This is what happens when we make ourselves slaves to the clock.

I am sure you are familiar with this internal dialogue: "Got to check my email, got to return those three phone calls, got to meet with my boss, got to book my flight to the conference, got to call my daughter's math teacher, got to pick up my laundry, got to get some vegetables for dinner." How can you feel happy under this kind of pressure, driven by tasks and overwhelmed by a sense of urgency? How can there be room for happiness?

Speed tends to drive you into a panic state where you lose control. We all know the dangers of going too fast. You make more mistakes and can spiral totally out of control. Happiness evaporates as soon as you lose control of your life. This chronic sense of urgency, this panic, this hurry is indeed a disease as real and as dangerous as diabetes or cancer.

When you are constantly prompted by the relentless urge to move faster and faster, your physiology suffers. Your jaws become tight. Your muscles in all parts of your body become tense. Your blood vessels constrict. More energy is wasted supporting all this tension as the body chemistry changes. There is a shift from the parasympathetic nervous system, the system that nourishes and upgrades the body, to the sympathetic nervous system, which is responsible for responding to the outer demands of the environment. All of your energies go towards tasks and activities that have nothing to do with enriching your inner life and vivifying your soul, and you are light-years away from the zone of happiness.

Do you know what ventricular tachycardia is? It is a condition in which the heart is beating so quickly that it does not rest long enough to be filled with the blood that it is supposed to pump to the rest of the body. The heart is caught in the clutches of speed, so concerned with beating fast that it loses its connection to the whole and it begins to panic—galloping frantically, pumping faster and faster, never mind what its purpose really is. Ventricular fibrillation ensues, followed by cardiac arrest and death.

As is the heart, so is the individual. As individuals, we are intent on quickening our pace. As we do, we lose our effectiveness and become worn out.

It is time to recognize that speed is a trap. It is time to break the chains that bind us to this senseless and unsatisfying way of living. It is time to stop—simply stop and introduce a sense of harmony in our lives.

The next time you find yourself rushing through the day, stop and see if speed is controlling you. See if your activities are connected to your purpose. Stop and enjoy the process of whatever it is that you are doing. Be sure to enjoy the present moment. It is the only time you have.

If you constantly use the present to chase the future, you never get to enjoy the present—and you cannot be happy because happiness comes in the present moment. This realization is at the heart of true happiness.

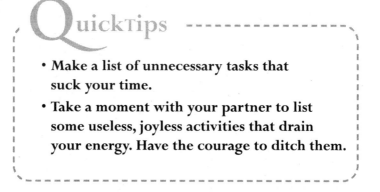

- **Make a list of unnecessary tasks that suck your time.**
- **Take a moment with your partner to list some useless, joyless activities that drain your energy. Have the courage to ditch them.**

Try these exercises—they may bring you more happiness:

1 In your imagination, take a helicopter and look down at yourself as you go through your day. Notice the way you function. See the whole picture and choose effectiveness over speed. Choose happiness over urgency.

2 Learn to wait. Don't just do something; stand there! They also serve who only stand and wait. Decide now that you will love to wait—and wait. Whatever your profession, the important part of your work is done by thinking, and this can be accomplished while you are waiting.

3 For the next little while, go into training to learn how to wait. And while you wait, increase your awareness. Try hard to heighten your appreciation of everything around you as you stand or sit and wait.

4 Choose the longest line in the drugstore or at the airport, keep your physiology calm, and move inwards and appreciate yourself

while you wait. You can also look at who or what is around you and give thanks for everything.

5 When you have to do something important, even if it is super urgent and has a deadline that you cannot change, don't just rush in and react to the feelings of urgency and anxiety that go along with speed.

6 Know the value of a pause. Wait long. Gather strength. Focus inwards and then move quickly. You may do less, but you will get more done. That is the paradox of speed. When you wait long and then move quickly, you will act with greater confidence, greater awareness, and greater power. You will simply be happier because you are more in control.

7 Stop what you are doing from time to time and look at your surroundings with an attitude of thankfulness. It will help you to focus your awareness and gain control of your time and your energy. It will help you to be happy.

R Quick Prescription 17

- *Recognize that speed is a trap. If you hurry too much you may never arrive.*
- *Put your time where the treasure lies and the treasure lies in you.*
- *Stop and enjoy the process of whatever you are doing.*
- *Choose effectiveness over speed. Choose happiness over urgency.*
- *Learn to wait. While you wait, practice focusing awareness. There is great value in a pause.*
- *When faced with a stressor, wait long. Gather strength. Focus inwards and then move quickly.*
- *Stop what you are doing from time to time and look at your surroundings and give thanks.*

The secret of happiness lies in savoring the moment,
in relishing every second with childlike, wide-eyed
enthusiasm. When you see an elderly woman sitting
on her balcony at five-thirty in the morning slowly
sipping tea and lazily gazing at the mountains
with a smug expression on her face, while you dash
off to the airport to attend another million-
dollar strategy meeting, know that you
have just witnessed great wisdom.
Envy it, or better still, try
to emulate it.
You have the choice.

18

HOW TO BEAT SPEED

- BEFORE RUSHING OUT OF BED IN THE MORNING, spend one rich, rewarding minute reflecting on who you are. Make a resolution to do this every morning. Take action to improve your life. Actually ask the two great questions in life: Who am I? and What am I doing here? Reflect on your values, beliefs, and special talents. Let them float to the top of your consciousness and act with them in mind. Please just don't read this—you will have wasted your time. Actions are the true indicators of what you really value and if you value yourself you will take action to ensure that you become a happier and more fulfilled individual.

- Before eating any meal, pause for 30 seconds to foster an attitude of gratitude. I myself take time before a meal to thank God and to ask for a generous heart so I can give to those who are hungry.

- Spend five minutes every morning reading something rich, something profound, something spiritually uplifting and intellectually stimulating—not reams of material, just a paragraph, a poem, or a quotation that can touch your soul and enable you to experience life from a greater depth of being.

- Soak in a bathtub for 15 lazy minutes at least once a week. Do it especially during your busiest times. Do it when urgency threatens to rule your life. That is the time to stop and head for the tub and regain control of your thoughts, your time, and your life. Leave some tasks undone. Remember that 80 percent of what we do is probably not necessary and if you nurture your life and your brain you will get the insight to know which tasks to tackle and which to neglect.

- Whenever the phone rings, use the sound as a cue to take two deep relaxing breaths and let all your muscles soften. Answer the phone on the third ring and treat it as a delightful interruption, not as an unwelcome chore that stops you from rushing.

- Introduce little pauses into your day, small rituals to remind you of what is really important as opposed to what is urgent. For example, make it a point to stop what you are doing, leave your workstation, and go say an encouraging word to one of your co-workers twice a day.

- Take five minutes out of your day to do nothing—just to throw away. Do it consciously. Defy the tyrant called speed.

- Use the 80/20 rule: 80 percent of what you do may be meaningless; pay attention to the 20 percent that is full of meaning. Find the 20 percent by constantly asking, "What is the best use of my time right now?"

- "Unbusy" yourself. It's not how busy you are that matters. Have you not noticed that everybody is busy? The CEO is busy rushing to the next board meeting. The lawyer is busy writing clever letters. The carpenter is busy repairing houses. The drug addict is busy collecting needles. The city bum is busy working the streets, and you are busy too. So what's the big deal? Refuse to be dominated by a frantic flow of activities. It's not what you do that matters but what you contribute.

- Move with awareness. Happiness is awareness. When the tyrant of urgency threatens to take your happiness away, slow down your movements, and focus on your body and experience what you are feeling. Learn to be still, for it is in quieting your mind and spirit that you will find strength.

- Set an energy-detection alarm. This will help you to be constantly aware of the state of your energy. When it falls below a certain level, the alarm will go off and you will stop depleting and start banking your energy by doing something that is self-enhancing and restorative.

- Introduce an attitude of play into your day. Try to find fun in every task you decide to tackle, however glum it may seem.

QuickTips

"Man is more nearly himself when he approaches the seriousness of a child at play." If you are too busy: bring a sense of play to everything you do and know that anything you do can be done with joy.

Quick Prescription 18

- *Spend one rich, rewarding minute reflecting on who you are.*
- *Introduce little pauses into your day, small rituals to remind you of what is really important as opposed to what is urgent.*
- *Take five minutes out of your day to do nothing. Defy the tyrant called speed.*
- *Ask yourself, "What is the best use of my time right now?"*
- *Refuse to be dominated by a frantic flow of activities.*
- *Move with awareness.*
- *Set an energy-detection alarm to ring in your head as soon as your energy is about to fall below the 50 percent mark, or below the desired level.*
- *Try to find fun in every task you decide to tackle.*

Relaxation is not something you do; it is something you allow to happen. If you want the benefits of a calm and balanced physiology, learn to let go.

Remember, letting go is hard to do. Practice it.

19

GET THE MASTER KEY TO THE KINGDOM OF PHYSIOLOGICAL HARMONY

PHYSIOLOGICAL HARMONY IS A STATE OF RELAXATION in which all the organs and systems of the body are functioning in a calm and congruent manner. It is an ideal state of readiness for action.

To unlock the door to physiological harmony, practice this simple exercise about 10 times a day, for as little as 20 seconds:

1 Shake your arms and legs briskly for a few moments to dislodge any tension that might have settled in your muscles.

2 Tense all the muscles in your body as tightly as you can without hurting yourself. Contract your facial muscles. Bring your shoulders towards your ears. Tense your abdomen and chest and tighten all the muscles in your arms, legs, and feet.

3 Take a deep, slow, even breath, and hold it for a few moments. Now breathe out and go completely limp and loose. Let all the tension drain out of your body. See it happening.

4 Continue breathing all the way in, and breathe out slowly and evenly all the way out. Bring your mind up your body from your toes as you breathe in, letting all your muscles loosen as you breathe out and extend the out breath to enhance muscle relaxation. Feel your muscles becoming more relaxed.

5 Focus on your arms and legs as you continue to breathe, and, as you breathe in and out, say, "My arms and legs are heavy and warm," and feel them becoming heavy and warm.

6 Continue to breathe consciously—in and out—deeply and slowly, and feel the gift of relaxation flowing into your arms and legs and spreading to your neck, shoulders, chest, and the rest of the body.

QuickTips

- **Beware of mind wandering and restlessness as you begin to relax. Keep on with the exercise and these distractions will eventually disappear.**
- **Remember that you are in training. Don't expect any quick benefits. It takes a while to change your physiology.**

R℞ Quick Prescription 19

- *Practice this relaxation exercise 4 times a day. You will eventually be able to do it in less than 20 seconds.*
- *With your jaws loose and your lips lightly together, breathe in through your nose and out through your mouth — slowly — three or four times. Do this several times during the day.*

Whatever you do for the highest good of others will always work out to your own highest good.

–Carlos Santana

20

BE A CONNOISSEUR OF
SEX, FOOD, AND DRINK

THE MORE I THINK ABOUT HAPPINESS, the more I am convinced that happiness comes from within. Pleasure, on the other hand, is of the body and can come from many sources outside ourselves.

An experience of pleasure can be so overwhelming and impact the physiology in such a profound way that it brings you almost to the border where pleasure turns into happiness. Thus, even if the pleasure comes to an end, the happiness you have continues long after the activity is over. Sex, food, and drink can bring you to that border where pleasure and happiness seem indistinguishable—but a lot depends on how you approach them.

For many of us, food is a great source of pleasure. How we consume it, however, can be a great source of unhappiness. I had a friend who used to say that eating is one of the nicest things to do. She ate to her heart's content and the more she ate, the more pleasure she got, but the less happy she became. So, nice as it is, eating cannot bring you happiness. Sixty percent of the population is overweight and yet only 20 percent of us would venture to say that we are happy.

Neither food nor drink can bring you happiness. Despite this, some people are able to get from a meal or a glass of wine or even a sip of juice such intense pleasure and internal delight that they are transformed into a state of ecstasy that can last for a long time. This is such a profound change in the brain and in the emotions that it approximates the state of happiness. I know a brain surgeon who is so enamored of food that his physiology lights up and his behavior brightens at the prospect of a delicious meal, and he even dances after eating. The feeling lasts and lasts and has such an intense effect on his mood that he seems to move beyond pleasure right into the arena of happiness.

Those who are profoundly affected by food treat dining with greater ceremony. They usually eat slowly, savor the taste, and connect the food to their health and function. Somehow they seem to expect more from food in a deeper sense, and they seem to get it. They seem to be able to extract joy from the simple act of eating.

The rest of us, on the other hand, tend to gobble down whatever we can find in an effort to appease our appetites. Any pleasure we derive from food comes from the act of eating and tickling our cheeks, and from eradicating the pangs of hunger. No deep sense of joy.

When I recall the behavior of my friend the neurosurgeon, I realize that it is possible to adopt such a holistic and ceremonial approach to food that the pleasure you get from it will last so long and be so complete that it affects not only the mouth and stomach but also the whole psycho-physiological state. This effect can be anticipated and felt, and the behavior that goes along with it is what separates the connoisseurs from the rest of us.

Likewise, sex is a source of great pleasure. And just like food or drink, once the urge has been satisfied, you are okay until the urge strikes again. Just as some people are able to turn the act of chewing and swallowing into an art that satisfies and inspires them in a holistic way, so great lovers are able to turn the act of sex into an art form that can profoundly affect the quality of the day, as well as the vibrancy of their relationships. How they do this is of great interest to those of us who get only physical pleasure from the act of sex.

The technique for turning the act of eating or drinking into joy and turning sex into lasting happiness is very similar. It involves being more conscious and being more present in the moment as well as being more cognizant of how what you are doing affects the big picture of your life.

QuickTips

Wherever you are, be fully there. When you are eating, drinking, or making love, take time, slow down your movements. Remember that the race is not for the swift nor the battle for the strong but for those who endure to the end.

I am going to give you a few practical guidelines that you can follow to get to that no-man's land where pleasure and happiness are almost indistinguishable. They are mainly concerned with sex. These are some of the attitudes that separate the great lovers from the rest of us.

If you want to become a great lover:

1 Think of sex not as an act but as a process that connects to your whole being, having the potential to lift your spirits and transform your relationship. Focus on the spiritual connection. Take a holistic approach to lovemaking.

2 Approach it slowly. Be present at every moment. Regard sex as such a big and powerful thing with so much to offer that you can't possibly do justice to it in a few hurried moments.

3 Know the prerequisites for good sex and fulfill them. I refer to hygiene factors such as privacy, positive regard for yourself and for the other person, and your own personal principles that motivate your behavior. Sex without that strong emotional connection is hardly worth the trouble. As a philosopher once remarked, in order to have sex you have to go out for a meal, then you have to come home, then you have to play a bit and then take off your clothes, and after all that you have to move. It's just not worth it, he says. But I can assure him that if the solid emotional magic is present it is worth every effort.

4 Make some goals that would benefit both you and your partner. When the happiness of another person is at the heart of an activity, the pleasure you feel tends to cross the border of the physical into the land of the mental and spiritual, where true happiness resides.

5 Use performance goals—especially if you are a male with the usual impatience and narrow focus. Set some mini-goals to govern your conduct and expand the experience. Tell yourself, for example, "I am going to engage in nonsexual contact for the first 20 minutes together. I am going to interrupt my movements occasionally and verbally express my love." Adopt your own goals, but, whatever they are, it is a good idea to have them influence your performance and bring it more consciously into the present moment.

6 Think of sex more as an expression of love or a celebration of life than the basic desire to appease your feelings. You must be able to honor your innermost being and devote yourself at the same time to giving pleasure to the other person for whom you seek here and after the highest good. If you cannot do these two things simultaneously, you need to rethink your actions.

R Quick Prescription 20

- *Eat slowly, savor the taste, and connect the food to your health and function. Eat consciously.*
- *Extract joy from the simple act of eating.*
- *Think of sex not as an act but as a process that can rejuvenate your body, mind, and spirit.*
- *Be present at every moment.*
- *Honor your innermost being and devote yourself at the same time to giving pleasure to the other person.*

DEFINITION OF HAPPINESS

Happiness is hard to define. In my clinics and seminars,
I have ventured to define love. I have ventured to define hope.
I have ventured to define pleasure. But I am at a loss to define
this inner glow called happiness. It is almost impossible to
put all that happiness represents in one short sentence.

Happiness is far more than the absence of trouble.

Happiness is more than getting what you want.
It is more than wanting what you have.

Happiness is more than appreciating the good
things that happen to you.

Happiness is more than love, for love brings its own
rumble of disquiet that can sadden the soul.

Happiness is more than gratitude.

And happiness is far more than contentment, for
contentment blocks daring and valiant actions and
thus robs you of noble memories of a life fully spent.

So what is happiness?

Happiness for me is a feeling that I cannot capture in words.
When I try to define happiness, I often quote a poem by
Proteus that some people use to describe love.
But it sums up what happiness is to me.

Happiness is something so divine, description
would but make it less;
'Tis what I feel but can't define; 'tis what I know
but can't express.

21

CELEBRATE EACH MORNING:
SAY HAPPINESS IS WHERE I AM

MITCH HAS JUST BEEN FALSELY ACCUSED of a vicious crime. His wife, whom he has loved for more than 29 years, is in hospital awaiting a major operation. His older son has just been diagnosed with a serious eye disease that could have disastrous consequences on his future. His younger son has had three operations on his brain and suffers daily severe headaches. His daughter is leaving home at age 17 to go to university more than three thousand miles away, and his mother, who has lived with him for more than 20 years, has recently lost her memory and presents a real challenge to Mitch. As if all that is not enough, a major decision just went against him in his bid to keep his business viable. He has to face the possibility of declaring bankruptcy. And yet Mitch insists that he is happy. As far as I can tell, Mitch is indeed a happy man despite all his troubles.

Not long ago I passed by a store on my way to pick up my son from an eye clinic. Out of the corner of my eye, I noticed a woman attending to a customer. This woman was beaming. The happiness she exuded was so compelling that I simply had to stop and take notice. As I watched the way she handled her customers, I knew I was in the presence of a very happy person.

Under duress of my feelings I entered the store on the pretext of buying some cleaning solution. As she served me, I observed her even more closely. She seemed genuinely happy and was so friendly and affable that I took the liberty of engaging her in conversation.

"Charlene," I said, reading her nametag, "You seem so happy. I noticed your smile from across the way. I am interested in the topic of happiness and I wonder if you could tell me if you are really as happy as you appear, and if so, why."

Immediately she said, "I am happy because I decided to be happy today, whatever happens. As a matter of fact, my husband has just had open-heart surgery, my mother recently died, and I am having serious financial troubles, but I decided that just for today I am going to be happy."

How is it that some people like Mitch and Charlene are able to summon, experience, and exude a feeling of happiness independent of the difficulties of their lives? Undoubtedly, the feeling emanates from inside, but it is as palpable as an enlarged liver or an oversized spleen. Yet its roots are so deep that the events of everyday life seem incapable of reaching to such a deep level of the soul to undermine it in any way.

This inner glow of happiness is something that few among us possess. Whenever I see it in any of my patients I stand in awe of it, for I know it is no consequence of luck, no side effect of wealth, no result of power. Many a man or woman has had all these and more, and yet yearns for a moment of happiness.

QuickTips

You carry your happiness with you on the mountain or in the valley. The simple fact is that happiness does not come from changing the outside. Happiness is not found but created on the inside. As William A. Ward says, "Happiness is an inside job."

In order to experience the kind of happiness that defies troublesome circumstances, I believe that you have to fan the flames of happiness when it is present so that when the wind blows, the rain falls, and times are tough, it will be so established that it will not be extinguished. This calls for a strong sense of discipline and determination to constantly take control of your mind and entertain happy feelings, even when it seems natural to give in to negative emotions.

Recognize that your happiness is sacred to you and you alone. You have to create and experience your own happiness.

Reserve a part of your soul, deep down beyond the reach of circumstances, as a receptacle for this thing called happiness. It is in this place that you will just appreciate who you are. It is here that you will reflect on the past with gratitude, face the future with hope, and enjoy the present moment as a festival of miracles. It is in this temple that you will identify with the universe and feel a deep, unutterable sense of joy at being part of it all—a joy that neither adversity nor disagreement can diminish.

If you develop your own internal experience of happiness, independent of circumstances, and nurture it with special attention, the events in your life will not determine how happy you are. You will always visit this inner spring from which the bubbles of joy will rise. You will always be grateful for the gift of life, always want to celebrate the universe—and that must be at least a taste of happiness. Try to program yourself in this way.

If happiness depends on circumstance, then circumstance can take away your happiness. But if you arrange it so that your happiness is so deeply hidden out of reach within the inner recesses of your soul, then only you can erase it. Remember that this kind of happiness, deep and enduring as it is, has to be programmed and then nourished day after day by some routine or rituals. You must do something to reinforce the feeling. Then happiness becomes an indispensable accompaniment of your very life, a joyfulness tied to the core of your being, and anything that causes you positive excitement is just a bonus.

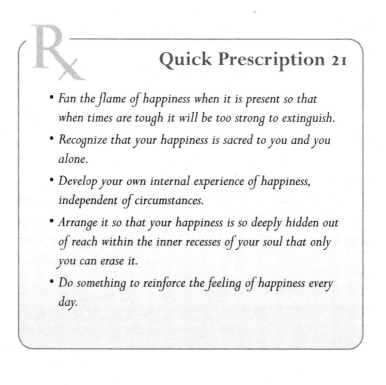

Quick Prescription 21

- *Fan the flame of happiness when it is present so that when times are tough it will be too strong to extinguish.*
- *Recognize that your happiness is sacred to you and you alone.*
- *Develop your own internal experience of happiness, independent of circumstances.*
- *Arrange it so that your happiness is so deeply hidden out of reach within the inner recesses of your soul that only you can erase it.*
- *Do something to reinforce the feeling of happiness every day.*

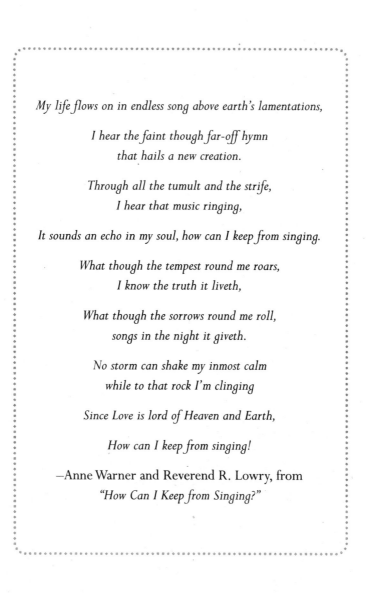

My life flows on in endless song above earth's lamentations,

*I hear the faint though far-off hymn
that hails a new creation.*

*Through all the tumult and the strife,
I hear that music ringing,*

It sounds an echo in my soul, how can I keep from singing.

*What though the tempest round me roars,
I know the truth it liveth,*

*What though the sorrows round me roll,
songs in the night it giveth.*

*No storm can shake my inmost calm
while to that rock I'm clinging*

Since Love is lord of Heaven and Earth,

How can I keep from singing!

—Anne Warner and Reverend R. Lowry, from
"How Can I Keep from Singing?"

22

MEET THE HAPPIEST PERSON
IN THE WORLD

WHEN PEGGY WAS FIRED from her job, her family and friends were devastated. They knew how much she needed the income, but Peggy was as cheerful as a duck. When asked why, she simply said she was lucky to have had a job that she enjoyed for so many years. And she looked at the positive aspects, such as finally having time to take a walk downtown and get to know one of the most beautiful cities in North America.

After years of wanting a baby, Peggy finally conceived at the age of 40. The little boy was always the apple of her eye. He gave her a purpose and, in time, she was the proud mother of an unusually well-behaved teenager.

At the end of a holiday weekend in New York, Peggy received a phone call just as she was leaving her hotel for the airport. It was the police, calling to tell her that her beloved son had been killed in an accident that morning.

Friends and family were at the airport on the other side to support Peggy in her sorrow. Peggy's first words were, "Thank God, at least I will get to see his body. Can you imagine how terrible parents feel when the child is missing and they never ever get to see and know what happened? Thank God, I know what happened, and besides I had fifteen beautiful years with this wonderful child. I just have to find the strength to deal with this terrible loss." And so she did.

Peggy's life is one continuous song of gratitude. Whatever the disaster, however copious the tears, Peggy is always thankful in the most sincere manner. She always looks for something to be grateful for. Perhaps it is because of her relentless gratitude that she is forever giving of her money and other resources. Not only is she the most grateful person I know, she is also the most generous, and she is truly the happiest. And yet, at face value, she has very little in the material world to be grateful for and very little to give.

I once saw Peggy leave an extremely generous tip for a waitress who provided only mediocre service. Her attitude was that the job of a waitress is hard; she, on the other hand, was lucky enough to just sit there and enjoy it all. She wanted to show her gratitude.

QuickTips

If you won't give a little when you are poor, you will not give a lot when you are rich. If you would like to give out of your poverty but you are waiting until you get more yourself, ditch the idea and begin to be generous now.

Since I met Peggy my attitude to life has drastically changed. I don't feel that anything is my right anymore. I feel immensely grateful to God for all the wonderful gifts He has given me. I have brains to enjoy thinking, feet to enjoy walking, eyes to enjoy seeing, emotions to enjoy relationships. Sometimes I slow down my movements just to notice my arms and my legs and to feel the gratitude for it all and for my connection to life. This is what happiness is all about. I want to give as much as I can to try to repay the world for the happiness I get from life—not that I ever could.

If you can do anything to brighten the universe, do it. If you can do anything to initiate and spread the feeling of joy to others, do it and enjoy the process. If you have both a one-dollar and a five-dollar bill in your pocket and you can afford to give the five-dollar bill to the crippled beggar at the corner, do it in style. Do it with an attitude of gratitude for the opportunity to spread a little cheer, and watch the response. Put a smile on his face and your happiness will soar. This is how Peggy lives her life and she is the happiest person I know.

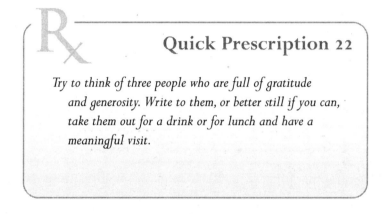

Quick Prescription 22

Try to think of three people who are full of gratitude and generosity. Write to them, or better still if you can, take them out for a drink or for lunch and have a meaningful visit.

He who has a why to live for, can bear almost any how.

–Nietzsche

23

LEARN HOW TO MOTIVATE YOURSELF

FROM TIME TO TIME, we all slip into a motivational slump from which there seems to be no escape. It is hard to feel happy at those times. As a patient once said to me, "Doctor, my get-up-and-go has got up and gone." This chapter is designed to give you a series of actions to bring back feelings of happiness and to keep your enthusiasm for life.

QuickTips

There are two kinds of motivation: the extrinsic one, fuelled by rewards and other people's praise and the intrinsic one that springs from the soul. Find out what motivates you to pursue your goals. Is it your parents, your lover, your kids, your boss, or is it an innate inexplicable love for what you do?

To jump-start your energy and get yourself back on track:

1 Renew your commitment to live more consciously. Open your eyes wide and really see what you are looking at. Likewise, really listen to what's happening, and hear what you hear. Actually hold your ears with both hands and pull the ear canals apart as a gesture

to remind you to listen more intently and to hear more clearly. Bring your senses more fully to your life and work.

2 Play some music that energizes you. Don't wait until it comes on the radio by chance. Take control of your motivation and play the music that will lift you up, and sing and listen to songs that will stir up your ambition and energy.

3 Examine your goals. Do you need new goals? Be absolutely clear about what you want. Look at the different areas of your life and ask the naked question, "What do I want?" Often the answer is nothing. That is why you are where you are. But if you keep asking the question, it will soon invade your consciousness and ignite your innate desires. Consider anew what you would want financially, what you would like to happen in your family, what you want your social life to look like, what you would like to achieve in your work, and what you want your relationships to look like. Begin to construct some new goals.

4 If you are facing a situation where a particular goal seems overwhelming, this might be a source of discouragement. Break it down into little steps. Apply the old adage, "By the yard it's hard, but inch by inch, it's a cinch."

5 Make a list of your whys. Why do you want this goal? Or, why should you get out of this state of inertia in the first place? "He who has a why to live for can bear almost any how." This is what Nietzsche said.

6 Review your accomplishments and count your blessings. Celebrate small achievements. Stop beating yourself up for what you have not done or what you do not have, and start congratulating yourself for what you have done and what you already have.

7 Visualize your goals accomplished. See the happy outcome in your mind. Use your imagination to help you succeed. "Imagine what you want, will what you imagine, and create what you will."

8 Regard your setbacks as temporary and not as permanent conditions. Maybe you are discouraged by a string of failures. Consider them as raw material from which outstanding success can be fashioned.

9 Treat obstacles as challenges to be overcome, gifts to make you stronger.

10 Mind your emotions. Get to know what you are feeling. Pay more attention to the emotions that surf through your body. Create emotions. As mentioned before, use music that you like to stimulate pleasant emotions in your body and mind.

11 Create an alliance with two or three other people and meet once a week to discuss your goals. Hold yourself accountable to these people for your progress.

12 Commit yourself to life-long learning. Always be in learning mode. Learning stimulates the brain. Learning lengthens life. The more you learn, the happier you are.

13 Go where something meaningful and motivational is likely to hit you. Expose yourself to different circumstances and ideas. Visit a science museum, a junkyard, or a church, and think.

14 Believe in yourself. Believe in your cause. Write down the main reasons for supporting your particular cause or organization and renew your faith in it. Belief is a powerful force and it is available free. Use it. Always believe with conviction that the things you want to happen in your life will happen. You can initiate your beliefs by writing them out and saying them with conviction and sincerity.

15 Exercise daily and eat wisely. From now on, be mindful of what you put in your mouth. You are going to eat consciously for health and energy, and not just to entertain your cheeks. In my experience as a doctor, there are very few people who do not know what to eat; the problem usually is having the determination to eat as healthily as you know how. Try to bridge the gap between what you know you should eat and what you actually eat.

16 Act the way you want to feel. If you want to feel motivated, act motivated. Put a smile on your face. Sit up straight. Relax your shoulders and feel energy flowing through your body. Act and speak as if you expect good things to happen.

17 Put humor in your work. Get interested in jokes and use them at work and at home. Laughing stimulates the brain.

18 Strengthen your spiritual connection. Look beyond yourself. Go to nature. Go to a place of worship and point your attention upwards. Connect your goals to your spiritual life.

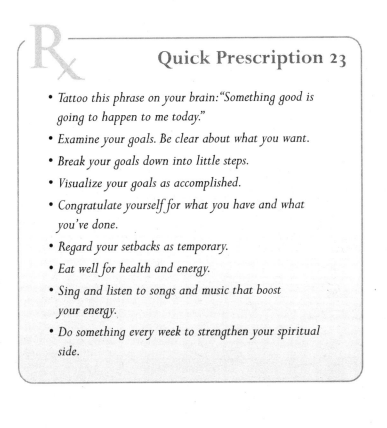

R

Quick Prescription 23

- *Tattoo this phrase on your brain: "Something good is going to happen to me today."*
- *Examine your goals. Be clear about what you want.*
- *Break your goals down into little steps.*
- *Visualize your goals as accomplished.*
- *Congratulate yourself for what you have and what you've done.*
- *Regard your setbacks as temporary.*
- *Eat well for health and energy.*
- *Sing and listen to songs and music that boost your energy.*
- *Do something every week to strengthen your spiritual side.*

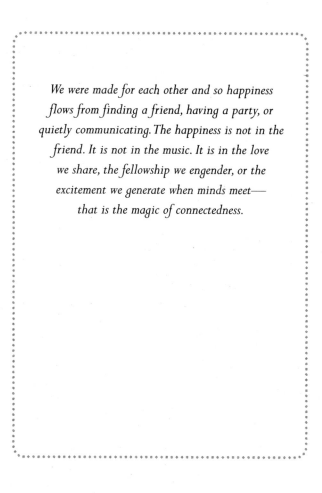

We were made for each other and so happiness flows from finding a friend, having a party, or quietly communicating. The happiness is not in the friend. It is not in the music. It is in the love we share, the fellowship we engender, or the excitement we generate when minds meet— that is the magic of connectedness.

24

KNOW HOW TO MOTIVATE OTHERS

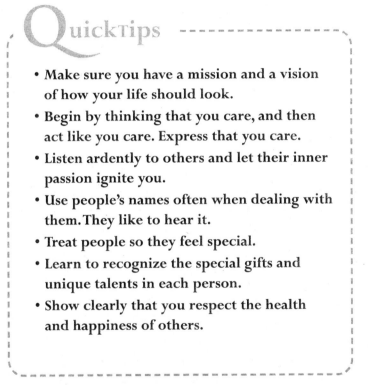

QuickTips

- **Make sure you have a mission and a vision of how your life should look.**
- **Begin by thinking that you care, and then act like you care. Express that you care.**
- **Listen ardently to others and let their inner passion ignite you.**
- **Use people's names often when dealing with them. They like to hear it.**
- **Treat people so they feel special.**
- **Learn to recognize the special gifts and unique talents in each person.**
- **Show clearly that you respect the health and happiness of others.**

HERE ARE SOME GUIDELINES **to motivate others and create a happier and more uplifting environment:**

Attention—Pay attention to the needs and wants of others. Behave with the significance of others in mind. Get in the habit of really noticing people. Be a "there you are" person and not a "here I am" person.

Belief—Believe in the individuals with whom you associate. Remember that it is people who make business work. Technology is a distant second. In order to create more happiness at work and at home, take the time to let people know that you believe in them. This will stimulate them to believe in themselves. And high-self-esteem confident people are happier to be around.

Care—Care is a verb. It is something we can all do. Begin by thinking that you care and then act like you care and say that you care. You can really affect others when they know you care about them.

Destination—When dealing with another person it is easier if you define the outcome that you are striving for, whether you are dealing with children at home or colleagues in the workplace. If you are ever in a position of leadership, make sure that you have a mission or a purpose that you are moving towards, and communicate this with people. Even in your home try to develop a mission for your family. You will notice a higher level of motivation and happiness.

Esteem—Forget your own ego and try to raise the level of self-esteem of others. Be a master at boosting the self-esteem and confidence of others around you.

Fun—Bring an attitude of fun and joy to your association with other people. Don't allow the mood where you are to become somber. Ask yourself the question, "How can I bring some fun into this?" And try asking this question at work and in your family when the atmosphere begins to darken.

Growth—Stimulate personal growth. Adopt a program of self-improvement and help others grow. Happiness is growth.

Hygiene factors—Support good working conditions, good pay, and the right tools. Show that you respect the health and happiness of others. Go out of your way to get this message across.

Insight—Provoke insight. Be a brain booster. Don't dump solutions on people. Lead them to insight. Help them create solutions for themselves and they will love being around you.

Justice for all—Beware of prejudice, favoritism, and inequality if you are in a position of authority. They are demoralizing.

Key result areas—Focus on a person's strengths. Learn to recognize the special gifts and unique talents of the people you associate with and cater to them. Ask yourself, for example, "What is it that Nicole can do really well? How can she make the biggest difference?" and pay attention to the answers.

Learning, laughter—Listening conveys respect. People like you when you take time to actively listen to them and show that you can learn from them. In addition to listening, learning and laughing are powerful tonics that boost brainpower.

Mistakes—Admitting error clears the score, and leaves you better than before. Be always quick to say, "I'm wrong and I'm sorry," and give people the freedom to make mistakes without trepidation in the work environment and at home. Learn to focus on what people do well. Remember the golden rule of management: What gets rewarded, gets done. Highlight what you want to see.

Names—Use people's names often when dealing with them. Everybody knows this, but we often neglect it. This is a reminder that people like the sound of their own names.

Openness—No hidden agenda. Let everyone be in on things.

Praise—Be hearty in your approbation and lavish in your praise. Notice what's good, and compliment. Celebrate.

R✗ Quick Prescription 24

- *Pay attention to the needs and wants of others.*
- *Let people know that you believe in them.*
- *Try to raise the level of self-esteem of others.*
- *Give people the freedom to make mistakes without trepidation.*
- *Be as transparent as possible.*
- *Be lavish in your praise.*

This is the one true joy in life,

*The being used for a purpose recognized
as a mighty one,*

*The being thoroughly worn out before you
are thrown on the scrap heap,*

*The being a force of nature instead of a feverish,
selfish, little clod of ailments and grievances
complaining that the world would not devote
itself to making you happy.*

–George Bernard Shaw

25

GENERATE HAPPY FEELINGS IN YOUR BODY AND MIND

SOME PEOPLE ARE NATURALLY HAPPIER than others, but your level of happiness, for the most part, is in your own hands. You can do something about it. I have found some techniques that work for most of my patients and if you practice even one or two of them, you will generate more happiness for yourself and for those around you.

QuickTips

When you notice that you are feeling unhappy, refuse to play the victim. Believe that your happiness is in your own hands and begin to do something to change the way you feel.

Here are a few practical ways to create happy feelings:

1 Exercise. If you do not already have an exercise routine, begin by going for a walk or a run every morning or evening. Begin slowly. You can start with 12 minutes a day and increase as you go along. Even if you are in a wheelchair, begin an exercise routine. Get proper clearance from your medical doctor and remember, don't try to exercise, just do it. Motion will trigger the flow of positive emotions.

2 Begin to live more consciously. Focus your attention more deliberately on yourself and your surroundings. Try to be more

discerning of what is in you and what is around you. Notice things. Notice how you feel in the morning. Notice what you put in your mouth. Notice how you greet your partner or your boss. Simply notice and you will gain more control. Awareness leads to control and control leads to happiness.

3   Change your diet. Eat with the knowledge that food affects your mood. Reduce your intake of refined sugar, consume less fat, and see if there is a difference in the way you feel. Do something about your diet. It may be something small like giving up french fries for 21 days, but take that small step. Most people know how to eat much better than they actually do and I am sure you are no exception. So just decide that now is the time to begin to eat for happiness. Get some information in this area if you need to, but don't delay. Take some action to improve the quality of fuel that you put into your machine.

4   Begin to use the intangible assets that are available to all of us, and which only a few of us capitalize on. Use belief, expectation, hope, intention, and attitude. Believe that your life will change for the better and intend to change it for the better. Then adopt the attitude of a more motivated and happy individual, even though you are still in the dumps. Believe that you are here to do something wonderful with your life. This belief is powerful, and yet it is free.

5   Begin to ask yourself more often why you are on the planet. Constantly prompt yourself to uncover what your real purpose is (I know I have mentioned this over and over). Keep asking the question, "Why am I here?" and take the question with you wherever you go. Don't let up. Live the question. Soon the answer will begin to gel and a sense of joy will ensue.

6   Make some goals for the different areas of your life. You can begin by asking yourself what you would like to be, what you would like to do, what you would like to see, what you would like to have, and whom you would like to help achieve more happiness and success.

7   Write down seven reasons why you should have a happier life.

8 Carry around a head full of positive images of what you want to happen in your life—not what is happening, but what you want to happen.

9 Create your own university. You are your own best teacher, says Warren Bennis, author of *On Becoming a Leader*. Construct your own learning program and make learning a huge part of your day. Pursue the courses you need to excel in your line of work. Read. Listen to motivational tapes and attend seminars and lectures on how to improve your life.

10 Join a book club, or better still, form your own. Just ask four or five friends to meet with you once a month for about two hours to discuss a specified self-development book, which all of you should read before you meet.

11 Begin to improve your spiritual life. If you don't already do so, take at least one specific action to enrich your soul every week. It may be going to a church for an hour a week or going for a walk in nature alone.

R℞ Quick Prescription 25

- *When you are feeling low, try vigorous exercise to change your feelings.*
- *Bring a higher level of awareness to everything around you.*
- *Write down three things you will do to achieve your ideal weight or improve your nutrition; for example, leave the table before you're full, drink water instead of juice, eat nothing after 8 p.m.*
- *Carry around a head full of positive images of what you want to happen in your life.*
- *At the start of your day, set a goal to learn something new, and at the end of the day ask yourself, "What did I learn today?" and take note.*

The stones that critics hurl with harsh intent

A man can use to build a monument

–Arthur Guiterman

26

GIVE YOURSELF THE WONDERFUL GIFT OF FORGIVENESS

No MATTER HOW KIND WE MAY BE, or how carefully we may craft our lives, someone is bound to hurt us from time to time. When this happens we have a choice: to forgive them or to hold in our minds the intention to inflict appropriate punishment. We may even choose to actively wish that some little disaster would befall them as a recompense for their past behavior.

If we are in the habit of entertaining negative thoughts against anyone who commits a grievance against us, considering how often this is likely to happen, our energies will be consumed in supporting negative emotions and we will have less energy left to celebrate life.

When we are hurt, whether it is by an insult, a false allegation, or a physical wound, we need not make excuses for the perpetrator or deny the extent of the damage. We have to acknowledge that the aggressor has wantonly hurt us and that it is natural to have negative feelings in response. But we also have to recognize a superior option to obliterate the transgression and the accompanying feelings of revenge and negativity, and move on. If you want to be a really happy person, always choose this option. Always choose to forgive, not for the other person's sake but for your own. This is how you can experience the incredible freedom and lightness of being in the world. It is like deleting a lot of useless, space-consuming programs from your computer—you free up the processor to do what is important. Be quick to press the delete button when other people hurt you.

When you decide to forgive someone, do it wholeheartedly.

There is no such thing as half-hearted forgiveness. Make the perpetrator know that your forgiveness is offered full and free. Make it known by your words as well as your deeds. Know that you have extended the pardon by an act of your own will, and be able to testify that you have gone the extra mile to demonstrate that your forgiveness is real. Then, let it go and enjoy the freedom and weightlessness of the gift you have given yourself, the gift of forgiveness, without which your happiness would have been seriously eroded.

When you realize that your sister had tricked your late father into leaving the family home to her even though you were the major caregiver, call her and make the first move to reconciliation. Be totally prepared to lose every penny if you have to, but come away with your mental and spiritual health and be free of any negativity that will block happiness and health from permeating your life. Living in a mansion with negative thoughts and a quarrelsome spirit is hell compared with living in the corner of a room with love and peace of mind. This is what forgiveness can do for you.

When you go to work and see the office gossip-monger smiling coyly at you, forgive her for the false rumors she deliberately spread about your spouse. Have the courage to tell her that you forgive her. Hold no grudge, no hope of revenge, just let go, and move on.

David knows that his wife, Janice, had an affair with another man in the early years of their marriage. She has since repented of her mistake and is now totally faithful to David. She is really in love with him and longs to be forgiven. But David finds it impossible to forgive and keeps bringing up the ugly past. Today they are seeing a counselor, and David looks much older from being weighed down by this heavy load of resentment.

David should have realized that forgiving Janice has very little to do with her but everything to do with him. While he harbors memory and resentment about the affair, his mind is not free, cortisol is running wild in the bloodstream depressing the immune system and his health and happiness are being compromised. The great pity is that he had the power to set himself free from this burden of emotional turmoil.

QuickTips

Walk around with a hunk of forgiveness in your pocket and throw it at anyone who hurts you.

Forgiving is so rewarding to the forgiver that you should orient yourself and develop the skill and the psychic energy to forgive at the drop of a hat. That does not mean you are a walkover or a doormat. It means you are strong, and all human beings are equipped with a radar system that can detect psychological strength in others.

I have become a firm believer in the power of forgiveness. And I am sorry to say that it is mostly for selfish reasons: forgiveness pays dividends to the forgiver. It strengthens the immune system and is one of the traits of an effective person.

Forgiveness has power and happiness in it, and I intend to squeeze out every drop that I can whenever I can. I have learned to swallow my pride and I have discovered the incredible lightness of the gift of forgiveness. I hope you will as well.

Quick Prescription 26

- *Always choose to forgive, not for the other person's sake but for your own.*
- *When you decide to forgive someone, do it wholeheartedly.*
- *Develop the skill to forgive at the drop of a hat.*

I will pay more for the ability to get along with others than for any other single skill.

–Andrew Carnegie

27

BE HAPPY IN YOUR WORK
EVEN IF YOU HATE YOUR JOB

LET US SUPPOSE THAT YOU ARE UNHAPPY at work because you hate what you do every day. You find yourself doing things for which you feel no real love. And you even hate to be around the people you have to work with. You are slaving away as a bookkeeper, for example, when your real interest is in working with animals. Your soul is not in your work.

The ultimate solution for your unhappiness is to quit your job and find the kind of work that you love to do, the kind of work that is in harmony with what you feel is your calling, even if the monetary reward is less.

But here is the problem. How are you going to support yourself in the meantime if you quit your present job? What will you do until you find the perfect fit? Starve? Most people decide not to starve, and continue day in and day out working at a job they hate. They continue to labor without joy and often die of heart disease before they find their true calling.

What I want to impress upon you is that even if you know you are in the wrong job and you have to continue for a while, you can be happy in the interim. I know you dislike the people. I know you despise the tasks. But do not let this destroy your happiness. You may have to continue in the job for a given time. But don't put off happiness until the right conditions prevail. Be happy doing the wrong job. Your nervous system and your fantastic body and brain are too delicate to be subjected to feelings of unhappiness, bitterness, and resentment on a daily basis for any length of time. That is one sure way to bring sickness upon yourself. This will hasten the demise of your memory and ruin your immune system.

If it is necessary for you to continue in your original job just to keep body and soul together, keep thinking that the time to be happy is now, no matter what. Always keep this in mind and go on to create that happiness, even when life hands you the wrong circumstances.

The same thing happens in relationships. Some people are obliged (or so they think) to stay in a less than ideal relationship for a few months for practical reasons. It is January and they know that the house will be sold in June, or the divorce papers will come through in May, or immigration to Australia will be completed by September, so they make up their minds to endure misery until deliverance comes. I had a patient who developed cancer before deliverance came.

I see many patients every day who are wasting chunks of their lives like this—waiting to be happy tomorrow. A wise patient, Joan Desusay, used to say, "Never put off till tomorrow the happiness that can be enjoyed today." This does not refer to indulging in pleasures outside of yourself. It is not a license to engage in immediate gratification. This refers to the challenge of getting happiness from each moment of life, even if the environment or the people are wrong. Here is how you do it:

- Remember that when we talk about happiness, we are talking about happy feelings—pleasant and enjoyable sensations in the body and the mind.

- To a great extent your feelings come from your thoughts; therefore, think positive thoughts. Refuse to go to work thinking how awful your job is and how unfriendly the people are. Rather, focus on the positive things about the job, even if you have to invent them, and then try to help them to come to pass. Keep your mind on pleasant thoughts, and your feelings will be pleasant.

- Pay special attention to everything in your environment and to the feelings and attitudes that appear. Beef up your awareness.

See Chapter 30 to get some instructions on how to do this. The great news is that the more you use your awareness, the sharper your awareness will become.

- Decide to pay greater attention to the movements that pass as you do your work. Bring a higher level of consciousness to the people around you and notice how they speak, move, breathe, and work. Notice the details. Just using your mind in this way will add a little more challenge and enjoyment to your day. Refuse to act in a passive, unconscious manner. Change your attitude on the job. Become a more highly alert and interested person. Become interested in things and in other people even if they seem naturally to turn you off.

- Try to turn your boring job into a fun job. Introduce some challenges to match the skills that you have. Introduce order and structure in a job that lacks these features, and make some goals related to the job, such as finishing a certain task by a certain time or doing something as fast as you can using only your left hand.

- Focus on the job in a single-minded manner. Think of nothing else but doing a good job and see if you can become totally absorbed in it for a while.

- Become a detective. Look for anything that is good and accentuate it. Ignore the bad and always magnify the good things in your work.

- Destroy your enemies on the job by turning them into your friends. Make a goal, tell yourself that you are going to have these horrible people crazy about you in two weeks. Use the job as a training ground for how to get along with difficult people. Give yourself permission to be impressed by the slightest appearance of efficiency and let it be known that you notice it. Give positive feedback to others and a friendlier and happier atmosphere will be created.

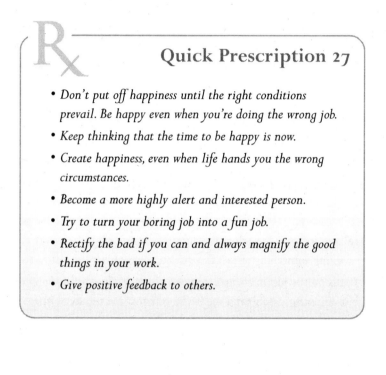

Quick Prescription 27

- *Don't put off happiness until the right conditions prevail. Be happy even when you're doing the wrong job.*
- *Keep thinking that the time to be happy is now.*
- *Create happiness, even when life hands you the wrong circumstances.*
- *Become a more highly alert and interested person.*
- *Try to turn your boring job into a fun job.*
- *Rectify the bad if you can and always magnify the good things in your work.*
- *Give positive feedback to others.*

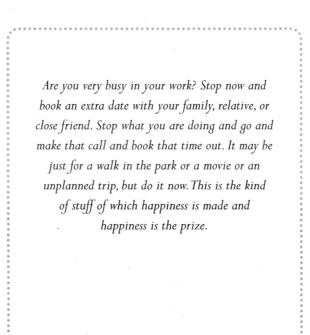

Are you very busy in your work? Stop now and book an extra date with your family, relative, or close friend. Stop what you are doing and go and make that call and book that time out. It may be just for a walk in the park or a movie or an unplanned trip, but do it now. This is the kind of stuff of which happiness is made and happiness is the prize.

28

REMEMBER MRS. HUMPHRIES

IT WAS ONE OF THE BUSIEST DAYS of my career as a physician. My office was packed with patients waiting to see me. It seemed as though everyone in the city was sick and I was the only doctor in town. I started my day by making rounds at the hospital. I was, however, so concerned with the large number of patients waiting at the office that I decided to put off seeing 87-year-old Mrs. Humphries until the next day, although she had specifically asked to see me that morning.

The next day I went to the ward to see Mrs. Humphries. The head nurse gave me a funny look and informed me that Mrs. Humphries had died an hour before my arrival on the ward, and that she had left an envelope for me. Right away I opened the envelope. It was a poem she had copied down in the final hours of her life entitled *Out of This Life* by an unknown author.

QuickTips

Are you too busy to lend a helping hand where it is really needed? The only thing that remains when you are gone is the help you have given and the love you have shared. As you give of your resources and share yourself, happiness soars.

Out of This Life

Out of this life I shall never take
Things of silver and gold I make.
All that I cherish and hoard away
After I leave this earth must stay.
Though I call it mine and boast its worth
I must give it up when I leave this earth.
All that I gather and all that I keep
I must leave behind when I fall asleep,
And I often wonder what I shall own
In that other life when I pass alone.
What shall they find and what shall they see
In the soul that answers the call for me?
Shall the Great Judge learn when my task is through
That my spirit had gathered some riches too?
Or shall at last it be mine to find
That all I worked for I left behind?

Quick Prescription 28

Visit someone in a hospital or a prison this week.
If you don't have anything to say, just be still and
give of your love and understanding.

You have not lived a perfect day until you have done something for someone who will never be able to repay you.

–Ruth Smeltzer

29

EXPERIENCE THE INCREDIBLE
JOY OF GIVING

IF YOU ARE AT ALL LIKE ME, you will find yourself more focused on what you can get from an experience, an activity, or a relationship rather than on what you can give. Most of the time we are not overtly conscious of how obsessed we are with what we can get for ourselves. It is just a quiet quality that runs deep in our lives. It is just the way we are for the most part. But the wisdom of the ages supports the position that there is far more joy in giving than there is in receiving. In my own life, the moments that give me a feeling of joy are the moments when I unselfishly give of myself or my resources. The major philosophers are crystal clear about this. They all seem to agree that it is better to give than to receive.

When I was in university, a girlfriend I really liked invited me to a rally for charity. When the donation basket came my way, I reached into my pocket for a dollar bill and to my great chagrin, a ten-dollar bill showed up. It was my grocery money that had already been spoken for, but I was too ashamed to slip it back into my pocket in full view of my girlfriend's admiring eyes. I had no choice. I ended up giving the ten dollars and was in pain for more than a month.

I wish I had known then how joyful giving could be, even sacrificial giving, if prompted by the right motive and executed with the right attitude. I would have paid less attention to my own needs and I would have experienced the rich joy that usually accompanies selfless giving.

I have since learned that joy is a faithful companion of giving when done with a willing heart. I was really impressed with what Ted Turner said after donating one billion dollars to worldwide charities: "This giving—I hope it gets contagious, because it feels good . . . I have never been happier than I am today." And this is what I am realizing as I get older. I am convinced now that giving is much more self-enhancing and elevating, much more vivifying to the soul, than getting. I am beginning to regret that I did not give more when I had the opportunity to do so.

If you stop to think about the simple phenomenon of giving, you will realize that all great men and women become great by contributing to a cause that is bigger than themselves. It is as if we find ourselves when we give ourselves to others. When we move beyond our own interests and get involved in the concerns of an organization or a cause, we take on a bigger and grander existence.

To serve means to connect meaningfully with others. It means that you are always reaching out, always poised and ready to give— and not only of your material possessions. To serve means to give of yourself, however and wherever you can.

When you give money or material possessions, you don't have to be emotionally involved, but when you give of yourself, you are acting from a deeper place and this triggers happy feelings that resonate from the soul.

Many millionaires who pay to feed thousands of homeless people still get out to the centers themselves. The satisfaction they report from footing the bill pales in significance to that which they receive from actually showing up and giving of their time and energy.

Get in the habit of giving of yourself—your time, your strength, your sweat, your brainpower. Do things for others without thought of reward. Do it wholeheartedly and passionately, and you will find yourself on the path to a happy life. One of the greatest regrets of my life is that I was not more generous along the way. I shudder to think of the great sense of meaning and joy I must have allowed to slip away day in and day out, when I was so intent on getting that I forgot to give.

I know a judge who delights in giving. His whole life is devoted to taking care of the poor even at the expense of his own needs, and the more he gives, the more his life seems to sparkle with joy. This man says that when you give of yourself, you are not just giving to the particular organization or individual. His view is that you are giving of yourself to life. You are responding to the highest call of the universe itself to do all that you can to serve the universe and its inhabitants.

This is the attitude that I now try to bring to my job. I try to see myself as a servant of other people. I work as if I am working for more than money, and in a strange way I get much more than money. When we adopt this expanded view of our function in life, we become more motivated and energized, and our rewards become bigger and richer.

QuickTips

- Ask yourself, "Am I missing out on the joy of giving? Am I more focused on getting than I am on giving?"
- Give away something valuable today, even if it hurts.
- If you are not sure that you should give away something because you may need it, pass it on and experience the incredible joy of giving.
- Be careful that you are not giving in order to look good or to get something in return.

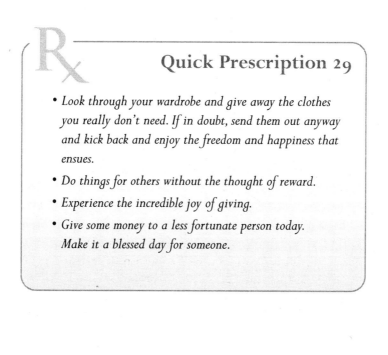

Quick Prescription 29

- *Look through your wardrobe and give away the clothes you really don't need. If in doubt, send them out anyway and kick back and enjoy the freedom and happiness that ensues.*

- *Do things for others without the thought of reward.*

- *Experience the incredible joy of giving.*

- *Give some money to a less fortunate person today. Make it a blessed day for someone.*

Boredom excites me. It offers me a unique opportunity to focus my awareness on whatever I desire and opens up a world of incredible possibilities. Focused awareness is the antidote to boredom.

30

TURN UP THE POWER
OF YOUR ATTENTION

THE POWER OF AWARENESS is one of the greatest gifts we have as human beings. It is a marvelous function of the brain. The fact is that we tend to take it for granted. As a physician I believe that the absence of awareness is a common cause of disease and discomfort. When we drift through our day and fail to take time to notice how we are inside and how our bodies are functioning, inside is dark, deprived of the light of awareness, and it is then that we can be easily overtaken by disease.

Attention has the power to transform our experience and change our physiology. The quality of our lives is a reflection of the quality of attention that we bring to ourselves as well as the circumstances around us. When you apply your attention to whatever you are involved in, life somehow becomes meaningful and your whole attitude changes. You begin to live with a greater sense of knowing and delight.

One aspect of the power of attention that really excites me is that when you pay attention to anything, your level of interest soars, and with it you gain a greater feeling of control and inner satisfaction. This concept is repeated over and over in this book and depicts my sincere wish that you grasp the fact that you can raise the level of your happiness by bringing a higher level of consciousness and more focused attention to your life.

If you are conversing with your spouse or a close friend and you find the encounter unbearably boring, you can increase your level of happiness right there and then. Deliberately begin to pay special attention. Notice where you are and what you are doing. Look at your hands. Notice what they are touching. Look inwards and really experience what you are feeling in a new way. Look at the other person as if you are totally captivated and listen. Listen delicately. Try to bring a new sense of wonder, joy, and delight to the experience by just paying attention in a special way, and you will soon find your level of happiness rising along with the level of your attention.

When we force ourselves to pay attention to the common experiences of life, we can't help but achieve richer, fuller, and happier lives, for happiness is largely the ability to find romance and enchantment in the common circumstances of life.

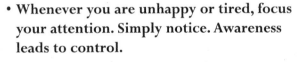

- **Whenever you are unhappy or tired, focus your attention. Simply notice. Awareness leads to control.**
- **Bring a higher level of consciousness to your daily life when unhappiness strikes.**
- **Bring yourself and all that you are fully to your life and to your work.**

Wherever you are, make a point of really being there. If you are listening to your daughter's account of her day at school and it seems to be wearing you out, bite your lip if you must, but begin to pay special attention. Open your eyes wide, make a tight fist, grip your socks with your toes, imagine yourself pulling your ears wider, and simply listen with great attention, and greater happiness will ensue.

As a function of the brain, attention improves with use. The more you pay attention, the more your attention will expand and the easier it will be for you to really listen and drink in the situations and circumstances of life. This is what wisdom is, and wisdom and happiness go hand in hand.

R Quick Prescription 30

This exercise will enable you to harness the energy of the moment. Not only will it make you happier, but also augment your success.

1. *Let all your muscles go. Loosen your facial muscles, let your jaw and your shoulders go, and relax your chest, back, and legs.*

2. *Pick an object in your view, or a thought.*

3. *As you breathe in, bring your attention from your toes up to your head, paying full attention to all the impulses in your body, and as you breathe out, focus your attention on the object or thought that you selected.*

4. *Do this five times, paying full attention to your body as you breathe in, and to your chosen object as you breathe out.*

5. *Keep breathing and focusing like this for a few minutes.*

   With practice, you will soon find an improvement in your brainpower and you will be better equipped to create happy moments in those uninteresting times when your mind begins to wander and your energy begins to fail.

If you want to be happy,

Begin where you are,

Don't wait for some rapture

That's future and far.

Begin to be joyous, begin to be glad

And soon you'll forget

That you ever were sad.

—Jo Petty from *Apples of Gold*

31

EXPERIENCE THE POWER OF GOALS

HAPPINESS DOES NOT COME BY ACCIDENT. It is never found. It must be created. The purpose of this book is to help you take action. Take your life in hand right now and become an architect of a happy and productive journey.

Think of the different areas of your life and consider what you really want to accomplish in those areas. Let your desires be profound, emanating from the soul. Establishing clearly what you want to do with your life is 50 percent of the battle. This is the power of goals.

In making up your goals, limit yourself to five to seven areas of your life and make up some written goals in each of these areas. Your health is one area where you should have some written goals—both physical and psychological. Your relationships should be another area. Your finances should be one. Your career should be one. And your spiritual development should be another.

QuickTips

- **Your goals should be personal and specific, motivational and measurable, ambitious and achievable.**
- **Take action today. Write your goals down.**

Having established the areas you want to target, use these 13 guidelines to construct meaningful, motivational goals to do it. I learned many of these steps from Brian Tracy, author of *Maximum Achievement*.

1   Decide on three to five things that you want to accomplish in each of these areas of your life. Be sure of your choice because once you designate it as a real goal, you are likely to get it. There is nothing worse than accomplishing a goal only to discover that it is the wrong goal.

2   Write down the goals and review them daily. Say them often. Your goals should be stated or written in the present tense and in the first person; for example, "I earn $5000 per month."

   If one of your goals is to be patient, repeating the words, "I am a patient person" or "I am becoming a patient person" is preferable to "I will be a patient person."

3   Examine the reasons you want these achievements. Make sure that they match your values and your sense of mission.

4   Set a deadline for their fulfillment.

5   Stay motivated and enthusiastic. Focus on fun. Approach your goals in an atmosphere of playfulness. Remember that solemnity is a disease. In Chapter 32 you will find many strategies to help you keep your motivation on a high plane.

6   Analyze your present position. Identify your strengths and weaknesses. Accentuate your strengths and attend to your weaknesses. Make your weaknesses irrelevant by compensating for them in some way. Consider getting help from someone who is strong in the areas where you are weak.

7   Determine the obstacles to achieving your goals. Devise ways of jumping over them or pushing them out of the way. Ask yourself, "What is the one thing that is preventing me from making the first move? What blocks the path to my success in achieving this particular thing?"

8 Make a plan of action. Put it in the form of priorities—what you will do first, what you will do next, etc.

9 Use your imagination vigorously. Visualize yourself as having already achieved your goals. See yourself as having arrived at your destination. Do this often. It is a great way to program your autonomic nervous system. When you visualize yourself with your goals achieved, you are teaching your brain to function in such a way as to attract the things, people, and circumstances that are in harmony with the goals that you have set for yourself.

James Allen says that the goal that you enthrone in your mind, the desire that you cherish in your heart, and the aim that you glorify in your soul are what you will live your life by, and what you will become.

10 Program yourself to persist when the going gets rough. Don't wait until you need persistence to call for it. Program it in your brain now. Tell yourself now that when you are tempted to give up, you will persevere. Keep repeating to yourself that, as far as your goals are concerned, quitting is not an option.

11 Keep your goals at the forefront of your consciousness. Inundate your mind with ideas that will encourage you to keep striving against all odds. Arrange your life in such a way as to include books, tapes, and seminars that will strengthen your resolve and keep you motivated. Have alliances with other success-minded individuals and meet with them often to exchange ideas. Take a great woman or man to lunch and learn from her or him.

12 Place a high premium on learning. Be always in learning mode.

13 Do at least one thing every day that will move you in the direction of your goal.

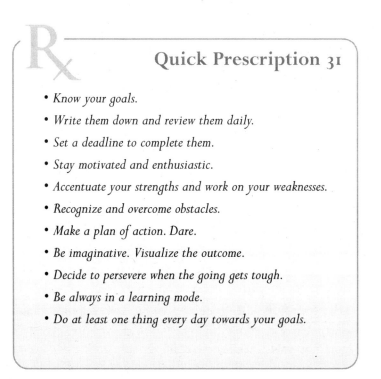

Quick Prescription 31

- *Know your goals.*
- *Write them down and review them daily.*
- *Set a deadline to complete them.*
- *Stay motivated and enthusiastic.*
- *Accentuate your strengths and work on your weaknesses.*
- *Recognize and overcome obstacles.*
- *Make a plan of action. Dare.*
- *Be imaginative. Visualize the outcome.*
- *Decide to persevere when the going gets tough.*
- *Be always in a learning mode.*
- *Do at least one thing every day towards your goals.*

Better to hunt in fields for health unbought,

Than fee the doctor for a nauseous draught,

The wise, for cure, on exercise depend,

God never made his work for man to mend.

–Dryden

32

CREATE A SUPER HEALTHY BODY AND MIND

MOST PEOPLE, WHEN ASKED IF THEY ARE HEALTHY, will respond in a perfunctory manner. They will look at themselves, and in the absence of any gross abnormality or significant pain, will readily claim the gift of health.

The truth is that even if you haven't the faintest whimper of discomfort, you can be carrying a serious disease. What is even more frightening is that you can be reveling in the fact that you have no pain or discomfort, and be hours away from a heart attack or a stroke. For the most part, we lack the skill needed to connect at the deepest level to the internal functioning of our bodies.

It is crucial that you learn to focus your attention on your body. Learn to listen to the whispers of "disregulation" so that you will be able to gain control and establish a state of internal harmony. Learn to ascertain how healthy your cells are. Take time to listen to the body. Listen diligently. Listen opportunistically. Listen ardently. In this way the body will not ever have to shout at you with some awful disease before you take note. Failure to focus your awareness inwards and listen to the quiet whispers of the body is a major cause of disease.

This vivid inner awareness of your state of physiological functioning is your best defense against stress. It is also a source of real inner joy. When you recognize that you are smart enough to take time out to listen to your body in the midst of all that comes and goes and thus protect your most valuable asset, you will feel good about yourself, and this feeling is at the center of a happy life.

Physicians are great at detecting the presence of disease. They can tell you how sick you are. When you move out of the context of disease into the realm of high-level wellness, how healthy you are is a more difficult thing to ascertain. This is in your hands.

If you are interested in achieving and maintaining high-level health, let me share an important concept with you. Internalize this concept. It states that health is much more than the absence of illness. Health is a continuum in which the body, the brain, the mind, and the emotions are as one, functioning quietly with a high level of harmony and efficiency. Furthermore, when you get to a certain level in the continuum of health, you begin to feel a connection to the universe that you didn't feel before.

QuickTips

Explore the three avenues to better health:

- **Use food as medicine.**
- **Exercise regularly.**
- **Practice a stress technique that works.**

When we say, "I am healthy," we are often thinking of health as merely a station or a platform that we arrive at. Cease thinking of your health in such a linear fashion. Health is not a fixed station or an immovable platform. It is a continuum of higher and higher levels of functioning and deeper and deeper feelings of joy. Each level contains more excitement and exuberance than the one below it. Know the level at which you are functioning right now. Simply give yourself a mark. Then aim to improve your mark. Meaningful awareness is the first step to positive change.

Quick Prescription 32

- *Learn to focus your attention on your body.*
- *Listen to the whispers of disregulation and discomfort.*
- *Think internal physiological harmony.*
- *Remember that health is much more than the absence of illness.*

A coach was once asked how he could keep his cool in the middle of a crucial game when the championship was at stake. Without hesitation he replied, "In my life, first comes my Lord, then comes my wife, then come my children and next comes my job. So if I lose, I still have a lot left over."

33

WHEN TROUBLE STRIKES, DO A REALITY CHECK

It was a beautiful Friday morning in Bordeaux. My wife, my three children, and I pulled up in our Westphalia van at about 10:00 a.m. and managed to secure a parking spot right in front of the post office in the middle of the shopping area. We walked along the sidewalk, admiring the decorations in the windows of the various stores, and then disappeared into the mall amid what seemed like a million other bargain hunters.

We emerged after a few hours, and I was beaming with pride. I had stumbled upon the sale of a lifetime, where I bought the nicest Italian suit that was ever made. I can't tell you how happy I felt on my way back to the van, as I looked up at the beautiful sky, admired the stores on the street, and imagined myself dressed to kill in this beautiful set of threads.

As I reached into my pocket for the keys to the van, I noticed that there were pieces of glass on the ground beside the right front window. To my great chagrin, I realized that someone had just broken into our van and stolen an expensive camera and some recording equipment. Immediately, all my happiness vanished and negative feelings poured into my consciousness. Suddenly Bordeaux did not seem very nice anymore. I was beginning to see it as a haven for thieves. I was full of anger and resentment, ready to blame my wife for suggesting a parking spot that was near the end of the building, and so my sweet feeling towards her was about to be affected. Then I raised my head and, not far away, I saw my children coming towards me with the love of my life, beaming with joy. It was then that I had a sudden revelation.

I realized how lucky I was to have such happy and beautiful people with me. My heart leaped as I watch them running towards me to share the good news of what they had bought. I was beginning to get happy again as I realized that the break-in was really a very small stressor in the scheme of things. And I did a reality check. "How bad is this?" I asked myself. "What is the worst thing that can result from this?"

As I did a reality check, I realized that the equipment was all insured and that things could have been much worse. In fact, the trip would not be at all affected.

I then asked myself what was good about my life and what needed to be done. I answered that I was lucky to have the love of an outstanding family and blessings too numerous to count, and that the glass needed to be replaced. And so I just made a detour to the mechanic's shop to replace the glass at the expense of the insurance company.

Take a moment to reflect. When did you last overreact to a stressful situation? How could you have handled it better? Make a decision not to react without the benefit of reflection, even immediate reflection.

So whenever you find your happiness being threatened by a stressful situation, remember to do a reality check:

1 Get the facts, just the facts. Ask yourself what exactly happened, how bad it really is, and what is the worst possible consequence of the difficulty.

2 Count your blessings. Ask yourself, "What's good about my life?" Focus on positive qualities and assets and appreciate them with a new sense of gratitude. It will decrease the stress.

3 Take appropriate action. Ask yourself, "What needs to be done?" and do it. Negative emotions subside in the presence of purposeful action.

R̸

Quick Prescription 33

- *Do a reality check when trouble strikes.*
- *Get the facts.*
- *Count your blessings.*
- *Take appropriate action.*

*A measure of disquiet is a divine gift. The hope,
which in your eyes, shines on a dark threshold, does
not have its basis in an overly certain world.*

–Marcel Proust

34

PROTECT YOUR HAPPINESS

I WANT TO TELL YOU ABOUT SOME TECHNIQUES that many of my patients use to stay happy in stressful times. If you are really interested in this business of feeling happy, it is crucial that you resolve not to allow any negative event, however disastrous, to obliterate whatever happiness you may already have.

Happiness is the mortal enemy of stress. Stress cannot stand to be around you when you are happy; that is why it is important to defy unpleasant circumstances and try to generate and emulate happiness in times of stress. Notice that I say defy and not deny. You have to acknowledge the presence and the significance of the stressors but decide to be happy right there in the heat of the battle. And besides, you will find that when you adopt happiness in times of stress, your brain will function better and you are likely to find more creative solutions to your problems.

I am sure you are familiar with the situation where you are quite happy, whistling along your merry way when, out of the blue, something unpleasant happens. In a flash, unhappy feelings flood your physiology, and you remain in the pit of despair for days on end. The stressful feelings can take root to such an extent that even after the situation is resolved, you find it hard to recover your happiness.

Difficulties and stressors are the stuff of which life is made, and if we do not develop the skill to deal with them, our happiness will constantly be at the mercy of every wind that blows or every twig that falls. You can avoid a whole lot of unhappiness by making the decision to cultivate happy feelings, even in the face of disaster.

Remember that happiness is easy to feel and easy to cultivate in favorable circumstances. In the absence of trouble, most of us who decide to be happy can be happy. There is no real virtue in feeling happy when life smiles at you. Even miserable people can experience twinges of happiness when all is going well. The real challenge lies in being happy in the presence of a demanding boss or an overbearing in-law or financial problems. You have to make it your business to protect your happiness with such discipline and internal fortitude that nothing will dismantle it.

If you have not already done so, let this moment be a moment of decision for you. Decide now that you will allow no predicament, however painful, no slander, however devastating, and no attack, however bitter, to reach into your soul and rob you of the happiness that you have put there.

If your happiness is to withstand the swings of fortune, it must be deeply rooted in your body, soul, and spirit. It is important to recognize what happiness really feels like. Notice it, embellish it, magnify it and do not ever take the feeling for granted. Savor the feeling of happiness whenever you feel even a pinch of it. If it brushes past you, grab hold of it and embrace it with all your might, and let nothing, but nothing, desecrate it.

Take time to concentrate on how happiness feels. Notice where in your body you feel this capricious and elusive sensation called happiness. Do you feel it in your chest, in your head, or in your eyes? Become so familiar with the feeling of happiness, whenever you are lucky enough to sense it, that you will be an expert in attending to your own happiness by strengthening it, nurturing it, and defending it from the enemies that sneak up to destroy it.

Simply noticing and staying with the feeling is a great way to grow it. Attend to it, just as a doctor or a nurse would stay with a patient and cater to his or her every need. The best way to cater to anyone is to notice them—to recognize their unique gifts and talents and respond to them as if they were special. Do the same thing whenever you think you are happy or approximately happy. Accentuate your happiness by giving it your undivided attention. The more you notice happiness, the more it expands in your life, even in times of stress.

I often remind my patients that the most powerful stressors in the world come on two feet and talk back at you. They can demolish your happiness in a flash. To quote philosopher Jean-Paul Sartre, "Hell is other people." It is therefore prudent for us to resolve not to let what other people do or say determine our level of happiness. We must embrace the reality that our happiness is in our own hands and we must do our utmost to protect it from the intrusion of any person or outside influence.

There is nothing terribly profound about this. The real issue is to practice it.

Quick Prescription 34

- *Resolve not to allow any negative event to obliterate the happiness you may already have.*
- *Never take the feeling of happiness for granted.*
- *Attend to your own happiness by strengthening it, nurturing it, and defending it.*
- *Grow your happiness by noticing and staying with it.*
- *Accentuate your happiness by giving it your undivided attention.*
- *Resolve not to let what other people do or say determine your level of happiness.*

*Happiness is a bouquet made from the flowers
that are within your reach.*

35

DECIDE WHETHER YOU WANT PLEASURE OR HAPPINESS

I WAS GOING UPSTAIRS TO MY BEDROOM one evening when I saw a small plastic bag containing six of my favorite chocolate bars perched on the edge of a small mahogany table, begging to be rescued. I pondered for a moment, and one voice said, "Get yourself a treat. You deserve to feel a little pleasure. Go on, treat yourself." Another voice protested, "Do you want pleasure or do you want to feel happy about yourself? How about your diet? These candies would make you feel good for a moment, you know, but will they bring you closer to or take you farther away from your goal of being a healthy and happy individual?"

QuickTips

When faced with any choices or temptations, ask yourself if you want pleasure or happiness. Pleasure is of the body whereas happiness is of the mind and spirit.

With that admonition from inside, I decided to ignore the candies and I focused on doing some sit-ups. After a while, I felt proud of myself and became really happy that I was able to muster the strength to resist the temptation. This feeling of inner satisfaction lasted a long time.

I remember that I was faced with a similar choice when dealing with a young doctor who worked in my clinic. He said something hurtful and rude, and it would have given me great pleasure to hurt him. I was in a position to make his way difficult. I was sorely tempted, but I renounced the pleasure inherent in inflicting appropriate pain and opted to forgive and forget. I realized that I denied myself the pleasure of defending myself with gusto, but I left the office with lingering feelings of intense pride and happiness.

There is no doubt that happiness is far superior to pleasure. It is more profound and it influences the physiology at a deeper level. I am sure you know someone who made a tough sacrifice early in their life and years after continued to reap feelings of happiness from that one choice.

The trick then is to develop the strategy to choose happiness over pleasure. To do this, you need to be a master of the body, a conqueror of the senses. You must be able to bring your natural instinctive drives under the subjection of your will and let the better decision prevail. This is how you bank happiness: by choosing what is significant over what is easy and pleasurable.

I have found that pleasure and happiness are very different. The call to pleasure is compelling but its benefits wither and die very quickly. Enjoying a pleasure is often like plucking a flower. The plucking and the withering are inseparable. But happiness wells up from inside and is a sustained, positive influence on the psychological and physiological dimensions of life.

The next time you are faced with the choice—pleasure or happiness—choose happiness, and remember that the strong jolts of pleasure rarely point in the same direction as the gentle call to happiness.

Quick Prescription 35

Choose what is significant over what is easy and pleasurable. Remember that the strong jolts of pleasure rarely point in the same direction as the gentle call to happiness.

Look around.
What changes would you like to see in others?
Begin by letting those changes appear in you.
Become the change that you want to see
in the world.

36

CREATE GOOD LUCK FOR YOURSELF

IF GOOD LUCK NEVER SEEMS TO COME your way, take note. You can change your fortune. Don't wait for the circumstances to change. Don't wait for anyone to come to the rescue. Create your own good luck.

Relinquish the idea that you can change other people. Give up trying to change circumstances over which you have no control. Stop fretting over how unfair your predicament is. Spend the time and energy working on yourself and thus create your own good luck. I am sure you have heard that good luck is 99 percent hard work. The only problem is that the work should be focused on you. The big reward is not in remedying the circumstances or changing the seasons but in changing yourself. Try to transform yourself into a person who attracts good luck rather than one who repels it. Prepare yourself for success with such unmitigated devotion that when accidents happen, they will always happen in your favor, and when nature wants to choose someone to do a great job, you will be chosen.

QuickTips

The more work you do on yourself, the more attractive you will be to others.

Work harder on yourself than on anything else in the world, for that is where the treasure lies.

Here are eight practical strategies to create good luck for yourself:

1 First, make sure that you are in good physical shape. Begin to create your good luck body and brain today. You just need yourself to accomplish this. Some individuals confined to a wheelchair are in first-class shape and can perform daunting feats. The difference between a great performer and the rest of us is that the performer trains regularly and prepares for great things to happen, while we just sail along at an ordinary pace expecting fate to come to our rescue and make us happy. Begin a training program to create happiness that will make you the model of good health. Honor your body with oxygen. This is about the best thing you can do to create good luck for yourself. Do not put it off.

2 The second thing is to know what good luck looks like to you. An offer of a job paying $5,000 per month might not be good luck to someone already earning $10,000 per month. So in order to have good luck, you must know what you want to become, what you want to do, where you want to go, and what you want to have. You must possess a clear idea of what you want your finances to look like, if it's financial luck you're after. The clearer and more precise your goals are, the more likely you'll attract the energy of luck to assist you. Right now, write down two or three goals that sum up your mission in this world, and keep focusing on them. This is a great way to attract good luck.

3 The third thing you can do is to prepare for good luck. Suppose you want to be a great businessperson or an accomplished concert pianist: the groundwork is the same—get into top form by preparing. Know what others don't know. Learn what others refuse to learn. Go where others won't go. Keep your aim steadfastly in view, and good luck is bound to hit you. When you are in top form you get all the breaks.

4   The fourth strategy is to become a master at relating to other people. You cannot afford to have people working against you if you want to attract good luck. You need to set it up so that people appreciate you and want to help you. The best way to do this is to appreciate them and make it your active purpose to help them achieve their goals. I am sure you will agree that relationships are not easy. We are all so different in so many ways that when we come together there is likely to be a clash. Therefore, internalize the fact that everyone has an agenda quite separate from yours. Accept that their point of view will be different because their experiences have been different. If you relate to people as though they're from a different planet with a different reality, you will learn to replace judgment and criticism with curiosity and understanding. These qualities are like magnets that will pull people to your side.

5   Strategy number five is to resolve to make the most of anything positive that comes your way. Focus on this. Be like a cell membrane that filters out the injurious substances and accepts the amino acids and other nutrients that support and enhance life. In other words, accentuate the positive and let the negative slip away without much recognition except what you might have learned from it.

6   The sixth idea is to flow with every moment. You create this flow by being conscious and by focusing on the moment to the exclusion of all else. To practice, stop right now and appreciate this moment of your life. Try being in the moment and saying thanks for it.

7   Seventh, seek out positive people who will lift you up and enhance your success. Reject people who just want to rain on your parade and drain your energy away.

8   Lastly, listen often to the deepest desires of your own heart. Listen ardently to the prompting of your spirit. Try to recognize what it is telling you, and favor this over the impotent wishes that flash periodically in your mind. Keep your mind on your mission and move courageously in the direction of that special dream, and you will discover the truth inherent in Virgil's proclamation that fortune favors the bold.

If you pay attention to these eight points, they will help you create good luck for yourself.

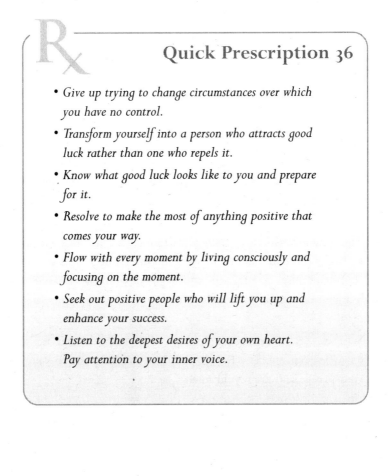

Quick Prescription 36

- *Give up trying to change circumstances over which you have no control.*
- *Transform yourself into a person who attracts good luck rather than one who repels it.*
- *Know what good luck looks like to you and prepare for it.*
- *Resolve to make the most of anything positive that comes your way.*
- *Flow with every moment by living consciously and focusing on the moment.*
- *Seek out positive people who will lift you up and enhance your success.*
- *Listen to the deepest desires of your own heart. Pay attention to your inner voice.*

The foremost task of any manager is to regulate his or her own energy and then orchestrate the energy of those around him or her.

–Peter Drucker

37

LEARN HOW TO
MANAGE YOUR ENERGY

NOT LONG AGO I HAD A 30-YEAR-OLD WOMAN in my office crying her heart out. She was not in pain: no misfortune had struck her family. She was crying because she had no energy. She was so tired that she could not read to her four-year-old son, let alone play with him.

If you are always exhausted, it is impossible for you to enjoy your life, however wonderful your circumstances may be. Your mind will be preoccupied with the feeling of fatigue and the heavy images that accompany it. Happiness will be the farthest thing from your mind.

At any point in time, your energy level is somewhere on a scale from 1 to 10, where 1 is low and 10 is high. It is your job to keep your energy at an appropriate level, compatible with the task at hand. At the end of the day when you are sitting and reading a book before going to bed, you don't want your energy level to be outrageously high, just pleasantly mellow. The trick is to always feel an abundance of energy over and above what you need. There should be a sense of physiological abundance—the feeling that you have more energy than you are using at the moment.

The key step in achieving this state of physiological abundance is to take charge of your energy and regulate it in a smart and efficient manner. You should strive to always enjoy that quiet state of readiness for more action than you are engaged in at the moment. It is the knowledge that you have the easy availability of energy to face what-ever comes your way that makes you feel good about being alive. This is a feeling that accompanies a refined and integrated physiology, which comes partly from eating right and exercising often.

When you are tired, all of your attention is focused on your physical tiredness and little or no energy is left to enjoy yourself. Therefore, since energy is always being used, it is crucial for you to learn to replenish your energy stores on a regular basis.

I like to think of energy in terms of an energy bank. Everything we do represents a withdrawal of energy. The fact is that we only withdraw—we don't deposit—and our energy account is almost always on the verge of being overdrawn. It is good to know how to modulate the use of our energy, how to conserve our strength, and how to build it up when it comes tumbling down.

QuickTips

On a scale of 1 to 10, rate your level of energy right now.
What can you do to improve your score?

Here are a few techniques to increase your energy:

- Set an energy-detection alarm in your mind. This will help you to be constantly aware of the state of your energy. When it falls below a certain level, let the alarm go off in your mind as a signal to stop depleting and start building up your energy stores.

- Turn the cells of your body into economic users of energy by exercising regularly—30 minutes, 5 days a week is a good way to achieve this. Make sure that it is medically advisable to do this. Get clearance from your medical doctor.

- Breathe deeply and slowly with complete awareness of your body and also of the process of breathing itself. Take deep breaths, bringing your mind up your body from your toes, and breathe out, letting all your muscles relax with profound abandon. Breathe like this whenever you remember.

- Punctuate your activities with rest. Don't allow yourself to become so tired and drained that you need to use extra energy to keep going. I once heard a surgeon groan throughout an operation he was doing on a patient's colon. He was trying by his groans to recruit the energy to keep going. Don't do that; plan your energy withdrawal better and stop before you drop.

- Listen to your body and respond quickly to the slightest onset of fatigue. You tend to create a more positive and energetic state when you change your activity regularly. If you are reading or writing a report, try to get up and break every 30 minutes or so. Upon returning, your energy, your memory, and your cognition will be improved.

- Practice differential relaxation. Differential relaxation is a neat skill that enables you to relax any muscle that you are not actively using at the moment and thus helps you to preserve energy. If you are typing at your computer, for example, you don't have to tense your neck or your abdomen. Yet most people do, especially when they are in a hurry. Differential relaxation offers you a way to relax your neck or your abdomen when other muscles that you are using have to be tight, like those of your fingers. Make it a habit to relax any muscles that you are not actively using.

- Watch your posture. Head high; eyes looking slightly upward; shoulders broad and loose; back, neck, and shoulder muscles relaxed. Let your head sit on your neck without any effort or tension and let your back sit on your pelvis and hips without any muscle contraction. Conserve your energy.

- Focus your awareness inwards. Be ready to detect the slightest onset of tension that rises from within and take action to eliminate it.

- Generate positive emotions by making your thoughts and your internal dialogue positive.
- Lastly, the most common cause of fatigue is not lack of sleep but lack of exercise. Make sure you get plenty of both.

R

Quick Prescription 37

Practice a technique called differential relaxation.
  Whenever you have a moment, tense your right hand as tightly as you can without hurting yourself. Hold the tension for about 30 seconds and while you are doing this, relax your left hand and all the other muscles in your body. Notice the difference between your right hand that is tense and the other parts of your body. Then relax your right hand and continue relaxing your whole body. You can repeat this as often as you like. You will over time increase your energy level as you learn to use only the muscles that you have to use at any given moment and relax the rest.

Breathing is the central rhythm of life—do it with awareness. When you are feeling nervous—breathe, smile, and relax. When you are feeling rejected or hurt—breathe, smile, and relax. When you are feeling happy—breathe, smile, and relax. Right now just for the heck of it—breathe, smile, and relax.

38

GIVE YOURSELF
THE GIFT OF RELAXATION

WHEN YOU ARE TENSE AND NERVOUS, it is almost impossible to feel happy. The next time you get into a rage or become acutely stressed, observe your body and try to decipher the emotions that you are experiencing. Right in the middle of the argument or the stressful situation, stop and ask yourself, "What am I feeling right now?" and see if happiness jumps to the fore.

Under stress and tension your muscles will be contracted, your sympathetic nervous system will be stimulated, your heart will beat faster and your blood vessels will constrict. There will be a general sensation of unexplained, erratic movements inside your body. These are the feelings that you will experience in this state of stress and tension. Happiness will have vanished or may be cowering somewhere in the background, while these other feelings dominate your sacred terrain. This is the promise of anxiety.

It follows then, that by learning the art of dispelling tension and nervousness, you are making it much easier for happy feelings to surface. When you relax you are taking a giant step towards increasing your enjoyment of life.

In a state of tension, your energy, in the form of ATP (adenosine triphosphate), which is how energy is stored in the body, is also being used up in maintaining unnecessary muscle contraction. Intrusive thoughts fly in and out of the mind; adrenaline predominates, causing more hyperactivity; and you become agitated and restless.

Relaxation is the antidote to tension. It releases the energy that is tied up in holding your muscles tight. It lets the muscles soften and shift into a quiet state of readiness for action. It also nourishes the brain, enabling you to experience the pure delight of clear thinking. This is the prelude to a positive attitude and pleasant emotions. For this reason, when you relax, your energy improves. You release ATP to the internal organs and your muscles are not using up all your refined energy in holding on to useless tension. Your cells are rejoicing because they find themselves in a pool of energy, much more than they can use. This is a state of physiological abundance.

QuickTips

Relaxation is the ultimate gesture of kindness to your body and brain. When you are relaxed you think more clearly. Whenever you are waiting for a meeting or an appointment, instead of just sitting there reading or reviewing your notes, take the time to relax. You will be better prepared for any eventuality.

When you are relaxed, more energy goes to your brain. Your level and quality of thinking soars and you can achieve much more than if you remained frantically busy and tense. In this state of relaxation you are not responding to feelings of urgency. You are not at the mercy of whatever comes or goes. You are prepared to face the challenges of your life in a calm and efficient manner.

Relaxation is an indispensable accompaniment to a happy life. It is therefore crucial in this stress-ridden world for you to know how to achieve instant relaxation and how to maintain a generally relaxed and balanced physiology.

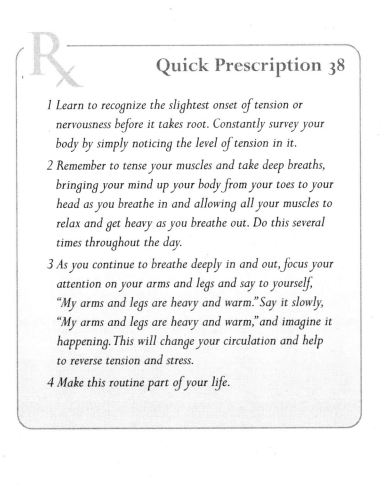

Quick Prescription 38

1 *Learn to recognize the slightest onset of tension or nervousness before it takes root. Constantly survey your body by simply noticing the level of tension in it.*

2 *Remember to tense your muscles and take deep breaths, bringing your mind up your body from your toes to your head as you breathe in and allowing all your muscles to relax and get heavy as you breathe out. Do this several times throughout the day.*

3 *As you continue to breathe deeply in and out, focus your attention on your arms and legs and say to yourself, "My arms and legs are heavy and warm." Say it slowly, "My arms and legs are heavy and warm," and imagine it happening. This will change your circulation and help to reverse tension and stress.*

4 *Make this routine part of your life.*

The single most important factor that will determine how long you will live is how happy you are.

39

LIVE SIMPLY

FINDING OUT WHO YOU REALLY ARE, what gifts you carry with you, and what's really in your soul, and then aligning your thoughts, attitudes, intentions, and actions accordingly—these are the hallmarks of a great person.

Many of us live our lives trying to conform to what others do or think we should do. We try to own what they own, to work the way they work—in the process we move farther and farther away from our true selves. This severely limits our ability to be happy. The more we think and act like ourselves, the more harmony we generate within ourselves, and the happier we become.

Happiness is not found in conforming to the norm. It is found in exploiting our own individuality and creativity. This is where authentic living starts. If, by force of habit or out of a desire to be accepted by others, you have been doing things foreign to yourself, decide that from now on you are going to be simple. You will be happier.

Be authentic. Be original. Be yourself. But remember you first have to discover who that self is, and this means that you have to spend time with yourself. Not with a book. Not with TV. With yourself.

Authenticity means having the courage to live to the best of your ability the unique life you have been given, with all its different twists and turns. It means refusing to contort your life into the mold of others for secondary gains. It means listening to your inner voice and living from the promptings of your own soul.

We often speak of an authentic antique. This means that it is not a fake in any way. It is true blue. It is without defect, or rather with all its defects but the defects are native to the thing itself. No patching up. You cannot turn a new table into an antique, although I have heard of some people who try to do that. An antique is simply the way it is. What you see is what you get. An antique carries its own style: no pretense, no energy copying another style.

And so must we be: simple, unadorned, uncomplicated, and true to our form. We must not introduce complexities in our lives to be like others. We must have the courage to be what we are and reflect what we are without concern for what others may think. As Walt Disney said, "The more you are like yourself, the less you are like anyone else, and that is what will make you unique. That is what will bring out the greatness in you."

I have a friend who is a surgeon. At one point in his life he felt the need to buy a boat. So against his own better judgment, he went out and bought a beautiful boat. I thought he was crazy. A boat was the last thing he needed; it just introduced unnecessary complication and expense into his life. Apart from the trouble of looking after it, he could never find the time to use it enough to justify its purchase. But the truth of it was that he could now say he had a yacht like many famous medical specialists in the city. He had to work harder to pay for it and to keep it well maintained. But all he got from it was the status that went along with being one of those lucky people who owned a yacht.

One day, after performing a long operation, he decided to drive to the harbor to show off his yacht to a friend. To his great chagrin, he found his wife enjoying the yacht with her new boyfriend. He has since decided to simplify his life.

As I get older I have learned that it pays to be simple. I try to peel away all the pretense, the façades, the antics, and the emotions of fear, anger, and self-doubt that I have for so long embraced. I sink down to my authentic, pristine self, because it is in being myself that I find happiness.

QuickTips

How much are you living the way you live because of what others might think of you? If it's not like you to throw parties and have a thousand friends around, don't do it because everybody else does.

Here are a few things you can do to simplify your life:

- Make much of the simple things—your time, your muscles, your heart, your brain. This will make you happy.

- Take care of what you have. It is often more profitable to spend time trying to keep what you have than trying to make more and allowing what you have to dwindle uncontrollably.

- Take care of yourself and your health. It is far better to live a simple and healthy life than a complicated and unhappy one even if your excuse is that you are trying to save the world.

- Ask yourself whether you are too busy. Drop some positions. Relinquish tasks and spend more time with yourself and your loved ones.

- Recognize what is most important to you. Do you find yourself neglecting the important people and issues in your life just to get a bit more money or a little better position? Renounce that attitude. Recognition in public life will not make you any happier if it is achieved at the expense of your home life.

- Resolve that you will never sacrifice yourself or your relationships for material gain.

- Spend your time and energy on what you value most. You will send a signal to your inner self that you are important and your life will sparkle with joy that emanates from within.

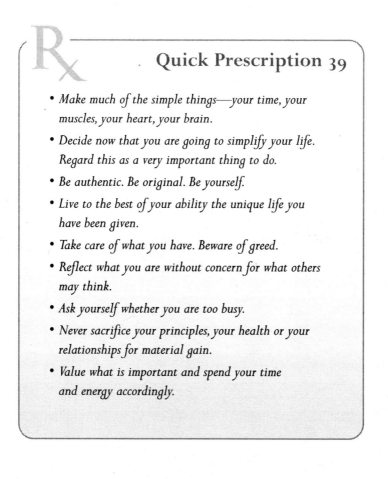

R_x **Quick Prescription 39**

- *Make much of the simple things—your time, your muscles, your heart, your brain.*

- *Decide now that you are going to simplify your life. Regard this as a very important thing to do.*

- *Be authentic. Be original. Be yourself.*

- *Live to the best of your ability the unique life you have been given.*

- *Take care of what you have. Beware of greed.*

- *Reflect what you are without concern for what others may think.*

- *Ask yourself whether you are too busy.*

- *Never sacrifice your principles, your health or your relationships for material gain.*

- *Value what is important and spend your time and energy accordingly.*

*Money is useless unless your know how
to turn it into joy.*

–Schopenhauer

40

PRACTICE TWELVE MORE WAYS TO SIMPLIFY YOUR LIFE

BEING SIMPLE IS REALLY BEING YOURSELF. You cannot really enjoy your life unless you know and own yourself. It is difficult to do that.

QuickTips

Peel away the trappings. Drop the negative emotions and attitudes that you have adopted and get down to your pristine, authentic self. Unencumbered, in stark simplicity, you will discover a wellspring of happiness.

We have to practice living simply and so I would like to encourage you to read through the following strategies and choose the ones that you feel can really transform your life.

- Know how much of anything is enough for you. A modest home may not be grand enough for your neighbor, but it may be perfect for you. There is always the temptation to please other people and live up to their expectations, but remember that you are unique. Beware of conformity. Value individuality. It is one of the pillars of a joyful existence. Recognize that how happy you feel and how satisfied you are in your heart is more important than how much you own, how much money you make or how much you are like other people.

- If you have the opportunity to work harder and acquire more, be sure you know what your striving is costing you in terms of wear and tear on your body. Your health is irreplaceable.

- Internalize the fact that happiness has very little to do with the accumulation of money and the stockpiling of material goods.

- Beware of greed. It has a way of severing the cords of compassion, according to author Richard Foster. When compassion goes, it takes with it the happiness and delight that come from caring and giving.

- Take at least 10 minutes every Sunday to review the list of values and principles that guide your life. If you don't have a list, make a list. Let the items on your list occupy a big part of your consciousness so that they can control your every thought and action and keep your activities focused on what really matters in your life.

- Refuse to be swayed by the relentless need to conform. The feeling that you have to be like others is one of the mortal enemies of happiness.

- Value your downtime. If you don't have any, create some and use it to get to know more clearly who you are. Also use your downtime to quell the incessant urge to conform and comply. Relax and be more like yourself.

- Take 5 minutes every day to be alone in silence and eliminate the restlessness. During these 5 minutes breathe deeply and evenly, as if you have all the time in the world and then try to carry this attitude of breathing into the rest of your life.

- Ask yourself: "Do I feel grounded, centered, and balanced?"

- Refuse to live beyond your means, both emotionally and financially. If you haven't any nerve left, why try to save the world and destroy your life at the same time? You will be much happier to simply be who you are and do what you reasonably can without a big strain on your heart.

- Don't let your spouse, kids, family, or friends persuade you to live beyond your means.

- Remind yourself every day that happiness is what it's all about. According to Ray Bradbury, you are here to celebrate the universe. You are here to know the gift. The best way to do that is to be simple.

R Quick Prescription 40

- *Recognize that how happy you feel is more important than how much you own.*
- *Know what your striving is costing you in terms of wear and tear on your body.*
- *Review the list of values and principles that guide your life. Do this once every week.*
- *Value your downtime.*
- *Take time every day to be alone in silence and eliminate restlessness.*
- *Refuse to live beyond your means, both emotionally and financially.*
- *Remind yourself every day that happiness is what it's all about.*

An aged man is but a paltry thing,
A tattered coat upon a stick, unless
Soul clap its hands and sing, and louder sing . . .

—W. B. Yeats, from *"Sailing to Byzantium"*

41

RECOGNIZE THE THREE PERSONS WHO LIVE IN YOU

WE ARE USUALLY SO OBSESSED with making a living that we ignore even more important aspects of ourselves. I hate to admit it, but even I, a physician with a special interest in preventive medicine, get so busy working that I ignore my health and have no time even to check my cholesterol or to sit quietly and think. Like many people, all my energies day in and day out are expended in tasks connected with work. This narrow way of life has caused me a lot of unhappy emotions.

If we are serious about being happy, we have to guard against this kind of imbalance in our quest for success. Don't get me wrong. It's okay to go after a great career, a beautiful home, a nice car and a fat bank account; however, we must leave room for self-development. We must take time out of every day to ponder the mysteries of life, and to reflect on who we are and what we are here to accomplish. This little time that you take to reflect will likely contribute more to your happiness than all the time you spend struggling to achieve financial success.

A family doctor in Oregon helped many of his patients achieve balance by giving them a system that I would like to pass on to you. According to his theory, there are three persons in every one of us: the male, the female, and the child. The male in us represents work—the drive to achieve and acquire, no matter what. This part of us is so domineering that, if given free rein, it would shut out any other influences, and we would suffer from imbalance and stress as other valuable aspects of our lives wither away.

The female in us represents relationships. This is the part of us that wants to ensure that we remain connected emotionally to our spouse, our children, our parents and our friends. This is the part of us that is concerned with love. Those of us who just work, taking no time out from our schedules to spend with family and friends, suffer from emotional deficiency. We can experience feelings of emptiness and numbness because we fail to cultivate love in our lives. In this state, our physiology is weakened and disease can more easily accost us.

The third person in each of us is the child. It represents play or fun and is always beckoning us to pay attention to joy and renewal. If this part of our life is neglected, we lose meaningful outlets for stress and we can become mentally and physically ill.

QuickTips

If you were being tried in court for lack of balance in your life, what evidence could you truthfully produce to the contrary?

Consider the following questions:

1 Are you obsessed with the notion that your work is your life? Is there any sense of balance in the way you spend your average day? Must you always be doing something related to money or work?

2 Do you spend time nurturing your relationships? Do you express your love? Do you tell your spouse, your kids, your parents, and even your friends that you really appreciate them? Do you deliberately take time out every day to listen to the people you love?

3   Does the child in you get a chance to express itself in play? Do you
know the incredible feeling of lightness to be fully engrossed in an
uplifting, meaningful activity that may not have any specific goal?
Do you take time out just to renew yourself or must you always
be doing something useful? Do you know how to relax and have
fun?

Examine these three important areas of your life. Ask yourself if you
are overcommitted in any one of these areas and make the appropriate adjustments.

R̷ Quick Prescription 41

*Create balance in your life by first creating balance in
your physiology. Exercise, eat foods that have great
value in fighting disease, and practice an exercise daily
to reduce the impact of stress on your body and mind.
Live mindfully.*

When I was working as an intern in Europe,
I took an afternoon off and visited a popular
square. I remember a young girl walking up and
down a short, crowded street, begging for money.
She told everyone that she needed to catch a train
to go home, but she had no money for the fare.
About a half-hour later the same girl was coming
up the street again. This time, to my surprise, she
was saying, "If anyone needs some money, I have
more than I need to get home." She was noticeably
more emphatic in trying to give back some of the
money that she had collected than she was in
collecting it. This really lives in my memory.
I guess I would have just grabbed the extra cash
and run. But here was a young person who
discovered at an early age that, even in her
poverty, it was more blessed to give
than to receive.

42

ASK YOURSELF IF IT IS WORTH DYING FOR

A YOUNG ACCOUNTANT had been working with a large manufacturing firm for seven years. He had his eye on the top job. Knowing that the CEO was nearing retirement age, the young man did all in his power to curry favor with the boss and bring himself to the attention of the board of directors.

QuickTips

Take a moment to answer these questions:

- **How much time do you spend daily with the most important person in your life?**
- **How much time do you spend with each of your children every day, giving that child your full attention?**
- **How much time do you spend with your spouse with your attention focused on just being together?**
- **If your spouse had a boyfriend or girlfriend on the side, are you absolutely sure you would know?**

The young accountant worked hard. He often stayed at work until late at night, leaving little time for his wife. He was almost a stranger to his five-year-old daughter. In order to compensate for his absence from home, he took his daughter one Saturday to his office. The little girl looked around curiously and then blurted out, "Daddy, is this where you live?" This was a great shock to him but not big enough to cause him to change. He continued in his old ways.

He had it all figured out: he was working to be appointed CEO of the company, and when that happened he would relax and spend time with his family.

One day he called the medical clinic and spoke in an ambivalent tone of voice. "I made it, Doc," he said. "This morning I was appointed CEO. But I feel a little pain in my chest, and I just want to check it out before I take over my new responsibilities. Can you meet me at the hospital?"

Twenty minutes later I arrived at the hospital. When I asked for the accountant, the emergency doctor informed me that he had just died. I knew about the sacrifices he had made and how much he had upset his family, but I did not know how much he had stressed his own heart. As I drove back to the office, I wished I had done a better job of warning him about the dangers of prolonged stress on the heart.

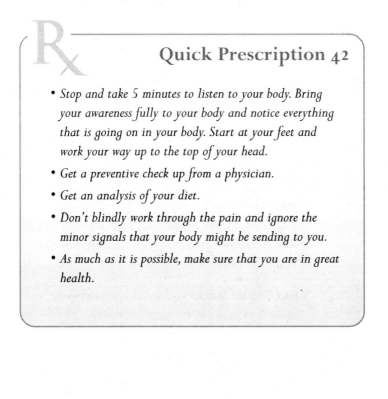

Quick Prescription 42

- *Stop and take 5 minutes to listen to your body. Bring your awareness fully to your body and notice everything that is going on in your body. Start at your feet and work your way up to the top of your head.*
- *Get a preventive check up from a physician.*
- *Get an analysis of your diet.*
- *Don't blindly work through the pain and ignore the minor signals that your body might be sending to you.*
- *As much as it is possible, make sure that you are in great health.*

"How do you know when the dawn has come?"
asked the Rabbi of his students. One student
replied, "When you can see a tree in the distance
and you can tell that it is an orange tree and
not an apple tree. That is when you know
that the dawn has come."

"Wrong," said the Rabbi. Another student replied,
"When you look in the distance and you can tell
whether an animal is a dog or a cat. That is
when you know that the dawn has come."

"Wrong," said the Rabbi. "You know that the dawn
has come when you look around and you can
begin to see that the people around you
are really your sisters and brothers."

43

TAKE NOTHING FOR GRANTED

ONE WAY TO BECOME A HAPPIER PERSON is to cultivate an attitude of gratitude towards everything and everyone. Decide that from now on, you will take nothing for granted. Try as much as possible to notice and appreciate everything in your environment. Learn to say thanks even when it seems like you have nothing for which to be thankful.

We tend to treat the more commonplace objects and experiences as part of the landscape; they go unnoticed, their unique benefits are overlooked, unless we decide to wake up and start paying special attention to the little things in our lives that mean so much. People who live together for a while begin to take things and each other for granted.

In my family, we have developed the habit of putting on an attitude of gratitude every morning. We actually imagine gratitude as an armor, which we put on in the same way as we put on our clothes.

The decision to take nothing for granted requires that you become more aware of the details of your life—the mundane, unpretentious details that we so often ignore. We must notice everything that is good and give thanks for it.

It is easy to feel grateful for something new or unusual that appears in your life. A gift of a new car would probably keep you thankful for months, but if you really want to be a happy person you must begin now to be mindful and appreciative of the old familiar things and the longstanding relationships in your life. Let not the smallest advantage go unnoticed or uncelebrated. Be grateful that the bus arrives every day even when it is a bit late. Be grateful that you have a way to support yourself even if you are looking for a better job.

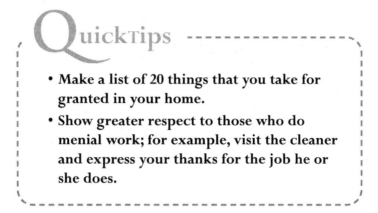

QuickTips

- **Make a list of 20 things that you take for granted in your home.**
- **Show greater respect to those who do menial work; for example, visit the cleaner and express your thanks for the job he or she does.**

I am sure you have heard the story of the prodigal son. It is recorded that he squandered his father's fortune and then returned home after many years. The father, touched and elated that his wayward son had returned home, threw a great party for him. This part of the story is good; it illustrates love and forgiveness. What is bothersome in the story, however, is that the father never threw a party for his older son, who had remained at home with him those many years. I often wonder if he took this older son for granted. Many of us do this. We go all out for our new friends and we treat the old ones with indifference. We take their faithfulness for granted and treat it as part of the landscape. We are respectful to women in general, but we never display any great awe for our own heroic mothers, who are always there for us.

This happens in love relationships all too often. We don't readily compliment our spouses on the daily tasks they accomplish, or the people they undertake to help, but we bend over backwards to congratulate others for doing far less. We choose to overlook the good that is so close to us.

If you want to cultivate more happiness in your life, begin now to notice things that have always been there but that you have never really seen. Bring a new sense of respect and gratitude to it all, especially the usual and the familiar. Put on some new glasses and see the world through lens of gratitude. Don't wait until you lose something before you recognize its value. Welcome the new, be impressed by the unusual, but never take the old and familiar for granted. See and appreciate its value.

For years I failed to notice what a terrific gardener my mother was. I lived with the results every day and became accustomed to having beautiful plants around me and a wonderful vegetable garden in the backyard, but I never made anything of it. I would tout the benefits of organic vegetables. I would encourage patients to avoid pesticides whenever they could, but I never really noticed that my mother was valiantly doing the same thing all along. I took it all for granted, and impulses of happiness that could have been generated and experienced were extinguished by mindlessness and indifference.

Who cleans the windows in your home? Go and tell that individual that you realize how difficult the job must be sometimes. Let them know that you fully appreciate their efforts and lighten up the atmosphere with appreciation.

Do you ever stop to say an encouraging word to the garbage crew? Now is your chance. Even if you have to wait around for them for a few minutes, it is well worth it. Let them know that you notice and appreciate their efforts. Shout it out from the patio if you must. Don't wait until they go on strike. Tell them and watch for the big smile you create.

Who cleans the floor of the building in which you work? Do you take it all for granted? Do you even know his or her name? Maybe you think that they get paid and therefore that is enough.

Here is an opportunity to create more happiness. Find out who does some of the more menial tasks where you work or where you live and express your appreciation. This is one way to increase the happiness in your own life, as well as someone else's. Don't wait till Christmas, do it now.

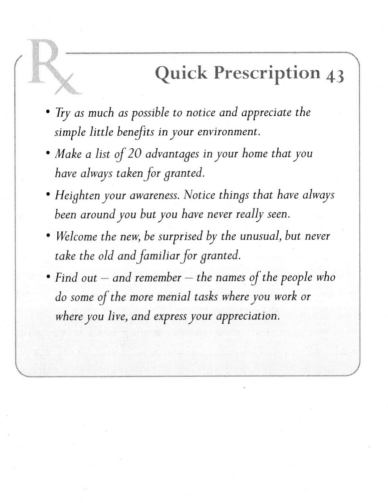

R︎ Quick Prescription 43

- *Try as much as possible to notice and appreciate the simple little benefits in your environment.*
- *Make a list of 20 advantages in your home that you have always taken for granted.*
- *Heighten your awareness. Notice things that have always been around you but you have never really seen.*
- *Welcome the new, be surprised by the unusual, but never take the old and familiar for granted.*
- *Find out — and remember — the names of the people who do some of the more menial tasks where you work or where you live, and express your appreciation.*

*Though the fig tree does not bud and there
are no grapes on the vine,*

*Though the olive crops fail and the fields
produce no food,*

*Though there are no sheep in the pen
and no cattle in the stalls,*

*Yet I will rejoice in the Lord, I will be
joyful in God my savior.*

–Habakkuk 3:17–19

44

BE HAPPY IN TIMES OF ADVERSITY

IF YOU HAVE JUST RECEIVED A RAISE, if the woman or man you are crazy about has just written you a passionate love note, if your favorite stock has just jumped to an all-time high, it is easy for pleasant emotions to flow. It takes no great effort to hold on to happiness at such times.

But what about when adversity strikes? Do we have the mettle to be happy in the midst of a problem or in the wake of some disaster? Can we feel a sense of peace even if something dreadful has just happened? The ability to be happy in the midst of disaster is the true test of a great individual.

If the events and circumstances of your life are particularly difficult right now and you can't seem to find any comfort in what is happening to you, remember that you have a choice. You can either match the unpleasant circumstances with an unpleasant attitude and a steady stream of gloomy thoughts or you can decide to invoke happy feelings despite what is going on.

What is interesting about the brain is that the moment you set out to be happy, even if you are in the midst of disaster, things begin to change inside. The process of thinking positive thoughts and adopting a bright and hopeful attitude will cause the release of neurotransmitters in the brain, which will jump-start the process of happiness right in the middle of the predicament.

Adversity needs not be a deterrent to happiness. The trick is to get your happiness so deeply entrenched within the soul, so much an

integral part of your daily living, that nothing should be able to erad-
icate it.

Take the first step. Right now even as you read this, decide that
you will not let misfortune take your happiness away whenever it
strikes. Carry your happiness with you whether you are down in the
valley or up on the mountain. Embrace this determination to be happy
no matter what happens. Program happiness as an antidote to adversity, so that when the storms of life hit you, your happiness will surface in full force.

Some patients have found that adversity, even in the form of a
medical problem, gives them an acute awareness of the beauty and
value of life. They report that they feel lucky and grateful. They get a
fresh revelation of how wonderful and meaningful their relationships
are. As they reflect upon this, right in the midst of the disaster, they
begin to feel a twinge of happiness rising up from within, even in the
dark corridors of the hospital.

When next you are hit with heartache, embrace the belief that
bad times can be a blessing. They can suddenly make you realize how
lucky you are and propel you into a joyful celebration of your life and
increase your appreciation for the love and support that you find.

Develop a plan to remain happy when hardship strikes, because it
surely will. Learn to deal with adversity in advance. Plan to throw a
hunk of happiness at it as you work hard to solve the problem. Since
life is basically one adversity after another, interspersed with short
periods of calm, preparing your mind to deal with calamity is one of
the best things you can do to ensure your happiness.

When it is summertime, go to the beach. Hike in the woods.
Enjoy the sun. Listen to the birds, but don't forget to think about winter. Use the good times to prepare yourself to be happy when the bad
times come along. Program yourself so that even if it rains or snows
you will be happy.

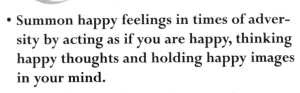

QuickTips

- Summon happy feelings in times of adversity by acting as if you are happy, thinking happy thoughts and holding happy images in your mind.
- When the going is rough, appreciate what's good about your life and what's good about you and dwell on those things.

Keep telling yourself over and over that you will let nothing stand in the way of your happiness. This is simple, but it is not easy to execute. You need to internalize it and remember it. Let the defence and embellishment of your happiness be second nature to you. To accomplish this you have to work on your mind. You have to practice holding positive thoughts in your brain and you have to learn to induce pleasant sensations deep within you, even when it is the last thing you feel like doing. This resolute determination is difficult to sustain but it will bring you happiness in the worst of circumstances and improve your personal effectiveness in life.

Try to develop a workable philosophy for adversity. Regard obstacles as teachers. Pretend that they have come into your life not to obstruct, but to instruct. See what you can get from them to make your life happier.

If you carry the right attitude and intention with you, difficult times will not take your happiness away. As a matter of fact, the opportunity to look for a better life, a new path, or a deeper sense of meaning may cause you to live more mindfully, and your level of happiness can increase even if the situation dictates the opposite.

Hope is a major part of the armor of a happy person when going through adversity. We should wear it, as Sir Walter Raleigh said, as a gown of glory. If you have just been handed the diagnosis of a serious disease, find comfort in what you have left. Find what is good about your life and celebrate that. Have hope in what you can do now to beat the diagnosis. This can actually add energy and meaning to your life. And the wonderful thing about the human condition is that the brain is not fixed. You can always improve. You can always learn to heal your body. This is the essence of the hope that you must stir up within you.

Here is a difficult command that is found in the Bible: "Rejoice in tribulation." Somehow this seems trite, but if you are going through a tough time and you focus on what is good about your life and what you need to do, you might find yourself happier in the process of getting through the disaster than you were before it struck.

The Roman philosopher Seneca said that the good things that belong to adversity are to be admired. Sir Francis Bacon reminded us that miracles appear most often in adversity. And the author Albert Camus summed it up best when he wrote: "In the midst of winter, I finally discovered that there resides within me an invincible summer."

Keep looking for your invincible summer even in the face of trouble.

R℞ Quick Prescription 44

- *Embrace the belief that bad times can be a blessing.*
- *Learn to deal with adversity in advance. Try to predict the hard times and anticipate and plan your way of escape.*
- *Use the good times to prepare yourself to be happy when the bad times come along.*
- *Use hope as part of the armor in the battle of life, especially when adversity strikes.*
- *Hope that tomorrow will be better than today.*

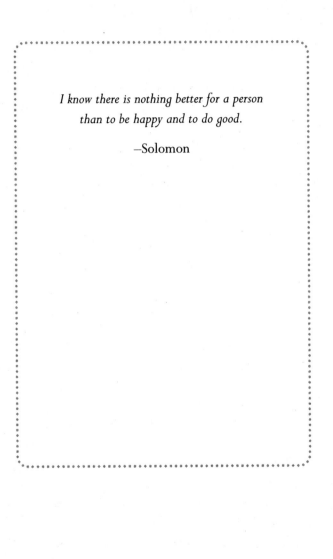

*I know there is nothing better for a person
than to be happy and to do good.*

—Solomon

45

GIVE YOURSELF
AN INTEGRITY CHECKUP

STACEY WAS A MANAGEMENT CONSULTANT with a very large firm that was in the throes of downsizing. She wondered every morning if today was her day to get the bad news. One day Stacey, her boss, and two other managers were having lunch in the company cafeteria. The conversation shifted after a while, and another manager named Jan became the target of some rather disparaging remarks. Stacey, however, believed in the principle never to be involved in a conversation where people were being maligned behind their backs. But in this case it was difficult for her to stick to her principle because her boss, in whose hands her employment rested, was the ringleader of the assault. How could she defend her principle and not run the risk of losing her job?

Stacey decided not to compromise her principle. She simply said, "Excuse me. I have a policy never to be involved in speaking ill of anyone behind his or her back. So I will just go and sit at the next table, and when you finish your comments about Jan, I will return." With that she moved to another table.

Two days later, her boss knocked at her office door. She entered and sat down, looking exceptionally sad. Stacey's heart was beating like mad. Suddenly her boss started to cry. "Stacey, something really awful happened to my husband. I have to talk to somebody, and you are the only one I can trust." Stacey's integrity had paid off big.

If integrity is not one of the parents of happiness, it must be one of its siblings. I know of no greater source of inner joy than the sense of congruence that comes from being true to oneself and living consistently with the highest principles of goodness. If you want to be a happier person, let integrity guide your every action. I often think of integrity as an inner sense of cohesiveness—a sense of wholeness that comes from oneness of thought, feeling, attitude, and action as you strive to live a life that is consistent with your highest principles.

When you practice integrity, every impulse pulls in the same direction. Without this sense of wholeness, you really are like a house divided against itself. You are torn and weak on the inside and it is impossible to be happy. With integrity intact, you get happiness from inner strength and you get to enjoy the pleasant sensations that accompany internal harmony. When you act with integrity you may not always get to do what is fun and easy, but you get to do what is important. This may be a hard road to travel in the beginning, but you will enjoy a deep sense of worthiness.

QuickTips

Integrity does not come after you. You have to go after it. The natural tendency of human beings is to lose integrity as time passes unless we do something special and deliberate to guard and enhance it.

If you are not careful, as time passes you will find yourself doing things that are inconsistent with your principles. Integrity is very moody. If you don't pay it enough attention, it will disappear, leaving you vulnerable to the temptations that so easily defeat us. Integrity is so tenuous and elusive that we can violate it without much effort. Dishonesty and shiftiness tend to sneak up on us, and, if we are not careful, we find ourselves breaking a promise that we made and lying about it to save face. It is so hard to tell the truth sometimes! Unless you resolve beforehand that you are going to tell the truth at all costs—and program yourself to keep the promises you make—you will find it impossible to keep your integrity intact, and you will miss the deep, enduring peace and happiness that integrity brings.

We all like to think of ourselves as people of integrity. But it is the way we behave in the trenches when the going gets rough that will determine if we do indeed have the gift.

Sometimes I find it unbelievably difficult to do what I know deep inside that I should do. Living a life of absolute integrity takes a lot of effort and, to tell you the truth, I feel like I am writing this chapter for my own good. I don't know about you, but I need to hear this over and over again to prevent myself from breaking one of my own rules. In the midst of a busy career, integrity can get lost. And yet it is the foundation of a positive and happy life.

I once heard Kenneth Blanchard, co-author of *The One Minute Manager*, say that there is no pillow as soft as a clear conscience, and I really believe that. Revisiting the issue of personal integrity from time to time is a great way to establish a firm foundation for your happiness in life.

I don't know if you have ever been in a position where you had to hide some of your actions from people who know you. Not illegal or immoral actions, but ones that were less than expected of you. It is a very uneasy place to be. Don't go there, and if you ever go there, don't stay. I can tell you truthfully that the people who have to hide some of their dealings from their employees or assistants are not very happy, even if they are making lots of money. There is nothing more disquieting to the soul than the fear that you may be found out.

If you have not already done so, decide afresh that you are going to practice integrity in every aspect of your life. You will fail from time to time, but if you make it an issue to have integrity as a priority, you will become a happier person.

I have found it helpful to adopt Kant's categorical imperative and use it in my daily life. Kant advised that you should behave as if, by your own will, your every act will become a universal law. That is like saying that you should act as if everything you do will be broadcast on the evening news as the decent thing to do. Would this change the way you behave? I have found that it has changed mine.

I don't have a television camera in my office, but since I adopted the principle to pretend that there is one recording my every word, every move, and every gesture, I think I have become more understanding, more congruent, more compassionate, and much happier. Maybe you could take an imaginary television camera with you to keep integrity at the core of all your actions.

R_x

Quick Prescription 45

- *Take a moment right now to write down the values and principles that are important to you.*
- *Decide to make integrity an overwhelming priority in your life.*
- *Let your actions be aligned to your highest and noblest thoughts.*
- *Take an imaginary television camera with you wherever you go and act as if it is broadcasting everything you do.*

If you want to be more than merely one of the masses, you must cease to be easy on yourself.

−Nietzsche

46

PRACTICE THE ART
OF SELF-DISCIPLINE

SELF-DISCIPLINE IS THE ABILITY to be hard on yourself. When you have the internal fortitude to put the desires and craving of your body under the subjection of your will, there is a sense of pride and confidence that wells up from deep within and you feel exceptionally good about yourself. Self-discipline leads to self-mastery and self-mastery leads to inner joy.

Discipline may be hard on you but its rewards are invaluable. Two-thirds of CEOs say that discipline is the preferred quality in any employee, and it has been labeled the master key to great achievements and riches.

Let us say that you know what your purpose is in life. Let us say that you have worthy goals to pursue. You have them written down and internalized. There is still a great gap between knowing what your goals are and achieving them. Discipline is the force that will close that gap. Sometimes the fear of punishment, ridicule, or being caught will keep you on track but compliance for these reasons will not yield the same satisfaction. The joy that accompanies true self-discipline is inspired from within.

One day while walking in Berlin, I dropped a few pieces of scrap paper on the sidewalk. I had been walking all day and was so exhausted that I was very tempted to keep going and ignore the mess I had created but I just had to go back to take up the pieces of paper and eventually throw them in the garbage. What was it that prompted me to do that? It was not because other people might have been watching me, I was too tired to care, but I just had to do it to be true to my own identity as a person who loves a clean environment. It was hard but I had the self-discipline to comply.

There are countless distractions from inside yourself, as well as from outside, that will keep you from pursuing your goals. You need a certain force to keep you on track, to keep you true to your commitment. This is where discipline comes in. Discipline will help you to respond to situations according to your values rather than take the easiest way out when difficulties and temptations come your way.

QuickTips

On a scale of 1 to 10, how high is your self-discipline? In what area of your life do you need the most help? For some it is in resisting the urge to eat. For others it is the discipline to exercise. Where can you use a little more self-discipline? Get ready to change.

Here are a few strategies that I try to use in my personal life as well as with patients in an effort to build self-discipline. Please try them.

- Decide that your every action should be an expression of your highest and noblest thoughts. Engage in activities that will have a positive impact on your life in the long run.

- When faced with the choice of acting in a way that will bring a deeper sense of long-term satisfaction or momentary gratification, always choose what will make you feel good about yourself in the long run.

- Keep your values and principles at the forefront of your consciousness and allow them to govern your actions. Don't put yourself in a position where you have to wonder how you should act under pressure; be so value-centered that you will always know what you should do.

- Distinguish clearly between pleasure and happiness. Learn to recognize pleasure as a fleeting feeling in the body as a result of something outside of yourself, and know that happiness originates from within. Many things can give you pleasure but only you can give yourself happiness. Can you think of an example in your own life where you got happiness from giving up pleasure?

- Surround yourself with books, CDs, DVDs, videos, tapes, and quotations about discipline. Keep reminding yourself that it is a pressing priority for you to become a more disciplined person. Remember that, like most virtues, if neglected and not fed, self-discipline will wither and die for want of nourishment.

- Listen whenever you have the opportunity. You will automatically become stronger inside. Listening is a wonderful resource for building discipline. Opportunities are endless and you don't have to pay a penny. Grab the chance to listen at every opportunity.

- Make a big deal of discipline whenever you see it in action. Notice it in others and learn from them.

- Resist the urge to blow your own horn. Discipline and humility are close cousins. They may even be sisters.

- Decide to entertain happy thoughts even in the midst of disaster. It takes great discipline to dwell on positive thoughts and images, and this is one simple way you can begin to practice self-discipline.

- Be slow to feel anger and resentment. He that is slow to anger is better than the mighty, says one of the wisest men that ever lived. Learn to step aside and allow anger that is aimed at you to pass by without affecting you. This takes real discipline.

- Exercise regularly. Develop a well-trained body, and this will give rise to feelings of peace, power, and internal fortitude.

- Look for opportunities to be around highly disciplined people.

Make friends with them whenever you can. Ask them what they did to become disciplined and listen.

- If you like peanuts, and you are not allergic to them, try eating only a single one from a bowlful that is right before you. Resist the urge for more.

- If you are trying to lose weight and have a huge appetite, always leave food on your plate especially when you really want it. Just say, better in the garbage than around my heart, and feel your long-term happiness soar.

- Practice being generous with your money and with your time. Cultivate the art of unselfishness.

R̲x Quick Prescription 46

- *Use discipline to help you respond to situations according to your values, rather than taking the easiest way out.*
- *Always choose what will make you feel good about yourself in the long run.*
- *Be so value-centered that you will always know what you should do.*
- *Distinguish clearly between pleasure and happiness.*
- *Listen whenever you have the opportunity.*
- *Notice discipline in others and learn from them.*
- *Practice self-discipline by entertaining happy thoughts even in the midst of disaster.*
- *Be slow to feel anger and resentment.*
- *Exercise regularly.*
- *Be around highly disciplined people.*
- *Resist the urge to indulge.*
- *Cultivate the art of unselfishness.*

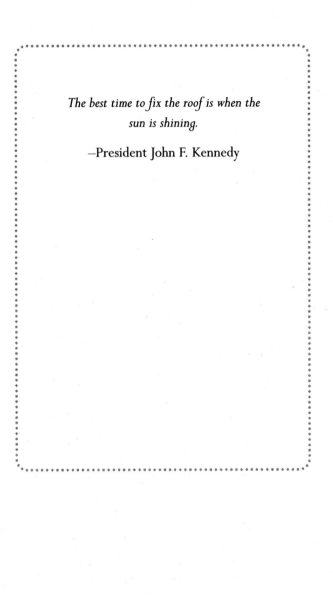

The best time to fix the roof is when the sun is shining.

–President John F. Kennedy

47

BEWARE OF GOOD TIMES

A YOUNG WOMAN WAS TAKING her father to her home for Thanksgiving dinner. While walking towards the house, they came upon a rough patch in the road and the woman immediately held on tightly to her father's arm to prevent him from falling. Whenever the road was smooth, however, she released her grip.

After dinner the old man scolded his daughter. "My dear," he said, "you have it all wrong. You see, when the road is rough, my feet have something to hold on to. I am most likely to slip and fall when the road is smooth."

After I read that story, I began to be extra vigilant whenever I found my path easy and smooth. I realized that it is when times are good that I tend to be complacent. It is easy to relax and throw caution to the winds when your career or your relationship is going well. It is in those very times, however, that you need to beware of slips and falls, even unexpected disasters. It is when you think that you don't have to pay attention that you are likely to lose your way.

I'm sure you're familiar with the saying that success breeds success. This might be so in some cases but in my own life, I have found that success breeds complacency. Success tends to make you want to sit back and take it easy, and it is then that disaster often strikes.

It is failure that breeds success. In times of failure you are more aware of your vulnerability and you are more likely to be careful. Failure puts in your hands the raw materials from which success can be fashioned. Tough times and rough roads are the elements from which a great life can be crafted.

If your life is going badly, you are usually more wary and you have good reason to work to make things better. When your life is going well, however, there is little motivation for improvement, and in your state of smug complacency you can be overtaken by a disaster lurking in the background.

QuickTips

On a scale of 1 to 10, how well is your life going? If you answer 10 or close to it, ask yourself what could go wrong and put some preventive measures in place.

When all is going well in your life, you should live consciously. Be careful with your money when you have a good job and no outstanding bills; it is exactly at such times that you are likely to make a serious financial mistake.

If you are in love and your relationship is working like a charm, be careful. Act as if you know that something is likely to go wrong and work to prevent it. It might sound crazy, but the period when you are feeling amorous and enchanted might be the best time to see a counselor and get some new ideas to enrich your relationship.

Use your smooth time wisely. Prepare for trouble while you have the luxury of a normal life. Summer is a good time to be thinking about winter. According to President Kennedy, the best time to fix the roof is when the sun is shining. The best time to do something about your future happiness is when you are already feeling happy. Don't let complacency be your downfall. Prepare for a happy life. Do it now.

Quick Prescription 47

Prevention is better than cure. Don't continue to do some-thing and enjoy it for the moment when you know it is going to bring you misery in the long run. Use the happiness you now have to give you the courage to make the break.

Give me my scallop shell of quiet,

My staff of faith to walk upon,

My cup of joy immortal diet,

My bottle of Salvation;

My gown of glory, hope's new gauge

And thus I'll take my pilgrimage.

—Sir Walter Raleigh

48

FLOW

MIHALY CSIKSZENTMIHALYI, the author of the book *Flow* and the recognized authority on the subject, defines flow as a very enjoyable state of being in which you are so absorbed in what you are doing that you lose concern for all else. Time, money, outcome, or what others might think of you are of no concern when you are in the state of flow. You are so intently focused that you become part of the activity. The experience is exhilarating, and you exist, for the moment, in a blissful period of time, and what seems like minutes can actually be hours. Here is where you do your best work. Here is where creativity and physiological joy abound.

If you could discover how to get flow in your work, you would be able to create happiness from the ordinary activities of your job, even if your tasks are repetitive and boring.

QuickTips

- **Ask yourself how much you are really enjoying what you do. Take a moment to reflect right now.**
- **Make sure that your activities are strongly connected to your sense of purpose in life.**
- **If you want more joy from the daily grind, prepare your mind to go into a state of flow more often.**

How do you get flow into your life? Practice some of these techniques:

1   Bring a higher level of awareness to everything you do. Even if it is something mundane such as peeling potatoes, wake up your brain and notice what you are doing. Pinch yourself if you must, but from now on, aim to be fully conscious. Wherever you are, be fully there.

2   Be clear about the goal of every activity you undertake. Know what you want the finished product to look like. Try to put a stamp of excellence on everything you do.

3   Apart from the goal for the end result, make a goal for the way in which you are going to do the job. This is called a performance goal. It will govern the way you function during the activity. In the case of peeling potatoes, your goal might be to peel them as close to the skin as possible, or as quickly as possible, or to peel six potatoes in exactly three minutes. The moment you introduce a goal into the activity, you increase your awareness and control, and the activity becomes more enjoyable.

4   Introduce some way to check your progress moment by moment. This is what we call feedback, and, in any field of endeavor, feedback is one of the major elements of enjoyment. Perhaps this is why athletes in different sports often get into flow. They call it "being in the zone." They have an outcome goal to win the match, but they also get plenty of feedback from the scoreboard as time goes on.

5   Focus on the task at hand to the exclusion of everything else. The ability to concentrate without distraction or diversion is the hallmark of great achievement, and you will be a happier person if you can apply this skill to the everyday tasks of your life. Focus on the process of whatever it is you are doing and aim to do it perfectly. Try to see yourself totally involved in the activity, as if you were part of it. Let go all concern and anxiety about time, about

what others might be thinking of you, about yourself, or even about the eventual outcome. Just focus all your attention on the task and you will get closer and closer to that blissful state of flow.

6 Assume control of whatever you are doing. Tell yourself that you have choices. Tell yourself that you are free to do this activity however you want and that you choose to do it well and with full concentration.

7 To create motivation and enjoyment in your work, always try to challenge yourself when you approach a task. Wherever possible, choose tasks that will make you stretch a little but that are generally within the range of your abilities. Match the degree of difficulty of any task with your level of skills. This will help you to focus your attention more sturdily. If you are bored, you may have to introduce higher levels of complexity or difficulty in your task, such as performing a particular chore with your eyes closed or with one hand as fast as you can. These techniques will tend to activate interest and increase your motivation.

R̶ Quick Prescription 48

- *Be crystal clear about what you are doing and what you want to achieve.*

- *Become a part of the activities in which you are engaged. Focus in a single-minded fashion. Whatever you do, do it with all your might. Wherever you are, be fully there.*

- *Bring a sense of wonder and joy to everything you do. Try to capture the enchantment in every task. Find the magic.*

Cont'd . . .

Quick Prescription 48 *Cont'd.*

- *Try as much as possible to do things that are significant to you. Do what you love and neglect what you don't love. Happy feelings depend to a large extent on what you decide to neglect.*

- *Care about what you do. Talk to yourself. Tell yourself that you care about whatever it is that you are doing. Care is a verb—an action word. Act like you care.*

- *Challenge yourself, even in your daily, mundane, repetitive tasks, to do them better or quicker or with greater ease and elegance.*

- *Set higher and higher standards for your own performance even in the simple, little mundane tasks. Aim to be the fastest and most elegant shoelace tier in the whole wide world, for example.*

- *Make sure you have the right skills for any task you tackle. Your level of skill must match the level of difficulty of the task.*

- *Watch your posture. Avoid any undue strain on your body. Notice if your neck or your back, for example, is being abused, and don't forget to breathe. Don't wait for pain or any warning signals to appear—attend to your body as a preventive measure.*

- *Be a relentless seeker of joy. Do not regard joy as something you will find separate from yourself, but as a prize you will get for living well—a feeling that will come to you as you do your job.*

A health unto the happy, a fig for him who frets,

It isn't raining rain to me, it's raining violets.

—Robert Loveman

49

BECOME MENTALLY TOUGH

MENTAL TOUGHNESS MEANS that you will be resilient in the face of difficulties and you will not surrender to the unhappy feelings that accompany the irritations of everyday life. If you are mentally tough, you will be the kind of person who can sing in the rain.

QuickTips

- **Do unpleasant people and difficult circumstances dictate how you feel on the inside, most of the time?**
- **Do you allow other people to spoil your day?**
- **Have you made the decision to enjoy your life and entertain positive feelings no matter what?**
- **Spend a little time contemplating these questions. Take a hard look at the way you react to people and things and make a decision not to allow anyone or anything at all to obliterate your happiness.**

Here are some practical steps that can make you mentally tough:

1   Identify your purpose. This is a recurring theme in this book and I hope the repetition will help you to take action. Go into solitude. I encourage you to do it today and ask the question over and over again, "Who am I and what am I doing here?" This is how you get the strongest and most resilient part of yourself to emerge.

2   Develop a positive mental attitude. Begin by writing down clearly what you want to be, what you want to have, what you want to do, and what you want to see happen in your life. Keep these things in the forefront of your mind. When emotions such as anger, resentment, fear, or worry appear, replace them with a strong desire to do something wonderful with your life.

3   Fill your consciousness with love, happiness, and hope. To fill your mind with love, think about the feelings and experiences that accompany love. Imagine loving scenes and act as if you love the people with whom you have to relate. These maneuvers will release feelings of love. To fill your mind with happiness, think about the times when you were happy and act as if you are happy. Smile a lot. Laugh a lot. Allow those happy feelings to surface in your memory. Act to make other people happy—make it your goal from now on to respond to others in a way that will make them happier than you found them.

4   Always expect good things to happen to you. Be an eternal optimist. Hope in the face of adversity.

5   Focus on these three emotions—love, happiness, and hope—and your mind will have no room for the negative emotions that tend to drag you down into the valley of despair and unhappiness.

6   Practice an exercise to induce relaxation and physiological harmony. You can use the workout in Chapter 19 to accomplish this.

7   Right now, why not reduce the tension in your body as you read? Increase blood flow to your arms and legs by thinking that your

arms and legs are heavy and warm. Try to feel the blood flowing into your fingers and toes right now. Breathe in and out in a balanced fashion, and allow your muscles to relax in a very profound way. Become acutely conscious of your breathing.

8 Adjust your posture. Move your muscles around and try to achieve a feeling of physical balance. This leads to a cohesive, integrated feeling that is very pleasant indeed. When you are able to achieve this feeling of being balanced and grounded, your happiness doubles, because, apart from the physical feelings that you create in your body, you will be feeling much better for having acquired the skill of self-mastery.

9 Think about the power of your attention in a new way. Regard it as a precious gift. Use it often. If you are sitting in a meeting and you are beginning to get bored, choose a word, a sentence, or a gesture, and focus your attention on it, and your brain will come alive again. Remember that attention leads to interest and interest leads to happiness.

10 Write down your goals. Make sure these goals are tightly connected to what you see as your overall purpose for being in the world. Keep your mind on your goals.

11 Decide that you are going to persevere to the end. Perseverance is the opposite of failure. This quality alone will make you mentally tough. To get perseverance, you don't pick it up when you need it. It is very heavy. You'll drop it again. Instead, program perseverance into your life right now—this minute. Just tell yourself with all your heart and soul and mind that you will persevere as you go after your goals, even in the face of grave obstacles. Imagine that the going will be rough, and tell yourself that quitting is not an option. If you program this invaluable quality in your life now, you will have it when you need it. It will be a habit of character, and, as you know, habits may be hard to acquire, but they are also hard to let go.

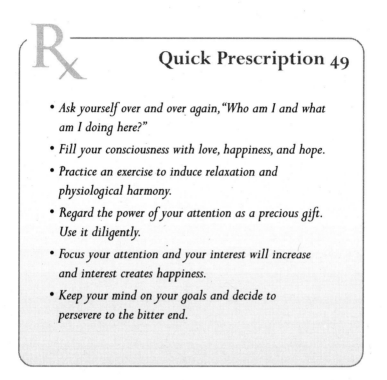

Quick Prescription 49

- *Ask yourself over and over again, "Who am I and what am I doing here?"*
- *Fill your consciousness with love, happiness, and hope.*
- *Practice an exercise to induce relaxation and physiological harmony.*
- *Regard the power of your attention as a precious gift. Use it diligently.*
- *Focus your attention and your interest will increase and interest creates happiness.*
- *Keep your mind on your goals and decide to persevere to the bitter end.*

As human beings, our greatness lies not so much in being able to remake the world, as in being able to remake ourselves.

—Gandhi

50

THINK GREAT THOUGHTS

THE FEELINGS THAT YOU NOTICE in your body come from the thoughts and images that you allow to occupy your mind. If you think great thoughts and hold pleasant images in your mind, you tend to feel great, even if you are in the midst of chaos. Thoughts are powerful. They can change the molecules in water and they can change your life. The quality of your thoughts determines the quality of your life. I am not just telling you to think great thoughts and leave you wondering, I am going to give you specific techniques that you can use to help you become a thinker of great thoughts.

QuickTips

- **Tell yourself that you are going into a special type of advanced training for your mind.**
- **Make a decision to practice at least one of these techniques everyday.**
- **It may be difficult at first but don't give up. Your brain cells will develop a new type of alertness and you will become a brighter and happier person.**

Here are the techniques to think great thoughts:

1   Think brain. We all use our brains, but, for the most part, we do so passively. We do not regard the brain as a part of the body that needs to be nurtured continuously. In order to become a thinker of great thoughts, we have to cease to take the brain for granted and become aware that we have an incredible instrument that is capable of unbelievable feats. Begin to notice the great potential of your brain and consciously bring its power to bear on the everyday situations of your life. Put your brain to the test, and you will be surprised how valiantly it will perform for you.

2   Eat in a way to enhance the performance of your brain. Most people know the dangers of a high-fat diet. They know that the arteries of the brain can be narrowed or clogged by a constant diet of excess fat. This can lead to tiny strokes, which will impede the power of your brain. This is why you should regard your knowledge of a good diet not as something you know, but as something you practice. Try to eat a diet that is low in fat, devoid of refined sugars. The carbohydrates you consume should have a relatively low glycemic index or low glycemic load. These are carbohydrates that do not immediately provoke the pancreas into sending a lot of insulin racing into your blood vessels; they tend to have less glucose than other carbohydrates. Your diet should also have adequate amounts of omega-3, which is good for the brain. You can get omega-3 from walnuts, flax seed oil, and certain types of fish, such as salmon, sardines, and herring.

3   Exercise at least six times a week for 30 minutes or more in order to increase the flow of oxygen to the brain. The quality of care that you give to your brain will determine the quality of your thoughts, and the more stimulated and effective your brainpower, the happier you will be.

4 Choose one or two significant thoughts centering on what you want to accomplish in life and stay with these specific thoughts as much as possible. Tell yourself that you are on the planet to fulfill a specific purpose and think about your purpose. Choose noble and lofty thoughts—not selfish or mediocre ones. Think about the kind of impact you would like to have on others, what you want your life to look like in two, three, or five years. Specific thoughts. Most of us think thousands of thoughts a day. These thoughts just glide in and out of the mind and are, by and large, impotent thoughts with no power to influence the course of our lives. What you need to do is to filter all the weak and unimportant thoughts out of your mind and attend to the one or two important thoughts that really matter.

5 Use your imagination constantly. It is a powerful tool. When pursuing a goal, imagine the process as well as the outcome. Try to follow your great thoughts through to their conclusion. Don't just see the big picture; don't leave your dreams hanging, follow them right through to the end in your mind. Don't gloss over the details, examine the details. That's where happiness is, right there in the guts of things, right there in the details.

6 Honor your thoughts with your intention. Intend to do great things. According to William Gladstone, a past prime minister of England, every one of us is capable of doing some great work in the world. Go through your life with a strong intention to do something wonderful with your life. When you invoke your intention, your physiology will change and your attitude and energy will become aligned to what you intend to do.

7 Beware of stress. When the pressures of life accost you, create physiological harmony. Breathe deeply and evenly, adjust your body to achieve a balanced posture and empty your mind by focusing on your breathing. Do it right now. Tense your whole body. Take deep breaths, focus on your arms and legs as you breathe, and try to assume a balanced position.

8   Rid yourself of all negative emotions. Easy to say but hard to do.
    Increase your awareness of your own thoughts and refuse to dwell
    on negative thoughts. Fill your mind with the one or two great
    thoughts that will make your life significant. Concentrate on how
    you plan to make your life count and begin to take action even if
    you are confronted with great obstacles.

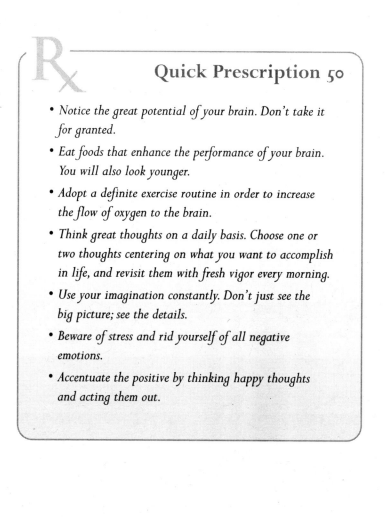

Quick Prescription 50

- *Notice the great potential of your brain. Don't take it for granted.*

- *Eat foods that enhance the performance of your brain. You will also look younger.*

- *Adopt a definite exercise routine in order to increase the flow of oxygen to the brain.*

- *Think great thoughts on a daily basis. Choose one or two thoughts centering on what you want to accomplish in life, and revisit them with fresh vigor every morning.*

- *Use your imagination constantly. Don't just see the big picture; see the details.*

- *Beware of stress and rid yourself of all negative emotions.*

- *Accentuate the positive by thinking happy thoughts and acting them out.*

The art of medicine consists in amusing the patient while nature cures the disease.

—Voltaire

51

DON'T LET YOUR AGENDA GET IN THE WAY OF YOUR PURPOSE

You will remember that we talked about how crucial it is for you to develop a vision, a mission and a definite purpose for your life. Regard this as something you must practice on a continuing basis. Go beyond the words. Be relentless in your search to find out what your life is all about.

Once you have an idea what your purpose in life is, aim to bring your thoughts, attitudes, intentions and actions in line with it. Refuse to engage in any activity that is in conflict with your sense of purpose. To the degree to which you can do this, you will experience a more profound sense of cohesiveness and inner joy.

Many individuals have gone through the agonizing process of questioning themselves day after day and have finally uncovered what their purpose is. They can tell you that their mission is to help the poor, to heal the sick, to clean up the planet, to educate children or to enliven the world with good music.

In my case, after much soul searching, I finally discovered that my over-arching purpose in life was not so much to heal the sick but to help people feel happier and more fulfilled. My mission as I see it is to bring as much joy as possible to everyone I meet. I believe, like Voltaire, that my function as a physician is not to heal the patient but to amuse the patient while nature does the healing. So, in my practice I have adopted the goal to put a smile on the face of every patient that comes through the door. But like most people, I get so busy trying to keep up with my calendar that I allow my daily agenda to get in the way of my real purpose.

QuickTips

Let your goals, your activities and the tasks that you tackle be guided at all times by your major purpose in life.

One Thursday afternoon while I was seeing patients in my office, I got a call from the hospital to come immediately to help the staff deal with a patient who was excessively stressed. I slipped out the back door, raced to the hospital and saw the patient in Emergency. Upon my return to the office, I was greeted by a waiting room full of anxious people. There was standing room only. Straightaway I hurried to see the patients as fast as I could. My agenda was then to empty the waiting room, but my real purpose in life was to use every chance I got to make people happy.

You would have been impressed with my efficiency as my agenda got the better of me. I called my first patient, made a quick diagnosis of degenerative disc disease, wrote a prescription and then moved on to the next one, who had pneumonia. I treated her in a flash and called in the next person. Patients flowed out of the office clutching prescriptions for every medication that was ever created. Then, with the waiting room still full, a woman who was about 40 was called in. She was embarrassingly heavy. She took about a thousand seconds to get up out of the chair. She took another thousand seconds to settle herself on her two feet and then struggle into the office, mumbling a few words tearfully under her breath. Before I could close the door to the consultation room, she collapsed onto the couch, took another thousand seconds to settle herself, reached into her pocket for what seemed like a long litany of complaints, cleared her throat and then began to address the first item on her list, entirely oblivious to the fact that the waiting room was full. She was slow of speech, and her effete, sluggish and inconsiderate attitude made me angry. My purpose receded into the background and my agenda took over. I hurried her along in a skillful manner. She didn't think much of my level of interest in her case and quickly thanked me and left.

Later that afternoon I discovered that this woman had come from another city quite faraway to see me because she heard that I could help her deal with a terribly stressful situation: her three-year-old daughter had been murdered by a mass murderer and she had come to me in agonizing distress. And that was how I had treated her. I allowed my agenda to get in the way of my purpose. When my ability to live on purpose was put to the test, I did what was easy instead of what really mattered. Please never let your agenda prevent you from honoring your purpose. From now on, resolve that you will always live and act and do your job with your purpose in mind. This alone will generate a deep sense of happiness and inner peace.

R Quick Prescription 51

Write down what you think your purpose is. Edit it. Then think about it and write it out again and again. Embellish it, visualize yourself accomplishing it and then try to do everything with it in mind.

Worry never climbed a hill

Worry never paid a bill

Worry never darned a heel

Worry never cooked a meal

Worry never took a horse to water

Worry never did a thing it oughter...

52

SUMMING UP

Happiness does not come in chunks. It is not measured in months or years. Happiness comes in moments. Try to internalize this concept.

QuickTips

Say "happiness comes in moments" over and over, and it will help you bring yourself more fully to the moments of your life and work.

There is nothing that tarnishes moments of happiness like worry. You are feeling great as you sit alone relaxing on your patio over-looking the harbor. Your husband has taken the children to dinner and a movie and you are experiencing a little piece of paradise as you drink in the silence. Then the phone rings. Immediately your happiness vanishes in thin air and worry rushes in to fill your the mind. As you answer the phone, your voice is already weak, your body is visibly shaken and your internal harmony is shattered. There was an accident. But it was so mild that everyone escaped without even a scratch. The car was only slightly scratched and the call was just to say that they will be a bit late coming home.

Instead of feeling grateful, you begin to actively worry. It is as if the phone call forced you to take off your happiness cap and put on your worry cap, for now you are worrying about what might have happened and what might happen in the future. Your moments of happiness are ruined as the giant of worry stands tall at the gate of your mind blocking any happy feelings from entering. The reality is that you have not only lost the present moment to unhappiness but you are likely to lose many future moments as well.

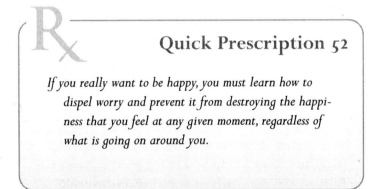

Quick Prescription 52

If you really want to be happy, you must learn how to dispel worry and prevent it from destroying the happiness that you feel at any given moment, regardless of what is going on around you.

What I want to impress upon you is that life is basically one disturbing event after another, and these events prompt us to worry.

Here are a few practical tips:

- **Remember that worry is useless** unless you learn how to turn it into joy. When worry approaches, don't fall prey to it. Focus your thoughts on the positive opposite. If you find yourself worrying that you might not get the job you just applied for, suddenly switch your thoughts to the fact that you are free and healthy enough to work towards getting an even better job. Think about that with passion and intense expectation, and remember you are free to think about anything you want. When you accentuate the positive in your thoughts, you begin to feel happier. As worry recedes into the background, making room for the happy feelings that have previously been barred.

- **If you tend to worry incessantly**, raise the level of your awareness. Set a worry detection alarm and when you recognize that you are worrying just shout under your breath, STOP!!! Then switch your thoughts to something positive and pleasant. Soon you will begin to worry again, but shout STOP once more and soon the intensity and frequency of the worry impulse will begin to diminish, giving way to waves of happier moments.

- **If you are worried about a specific issue**, like failing an exam you must take in two days or meeting your boyfriend's sister and wondering if she will like you, ask yourself, "What is the worst that can happen?" Think of the worst outcomes, such as, Will I die? Will I become blind or deaf or lose my home or my loved ones? Celebrate the fact that these things won't happen and begin to work hard to prevent the worst thing that is likely to happen from coming to pass. Don't worry about the worst thing happening; work to prevent the worst thing from happening. Worry melts in the presence of positive meaningful action.

SUMMING UP

Happiness! We can go on and on about it, can't we? But it's time to sum up and I want you to take away a few key thoughts.

- The first is to live your life knowing that happiness is relevant in all aspects of it. Happiness correlates with good health—as King Solomon said, a cheerful heart is good medicine. And recent studies have confirmed that, when you decide to live a happy life, your natural killer cells IGg, IGa, and IGm all increase. These are the armies that your immune system uses to defend you from disease. So, remember, when you make the decision to be happy, you are making a decision to be healthy too. No wonder Solomon concluded that there is nothing better for human beings than to be happy.

- Another point to think about is that you can make your own happiness even in the midst of chaos. Remember to take on the role of a happy person, and you will attract happiness.

- Even though we work to be financially responsible, the last key point I want you to take away comes from Schopenhauer: money is useless unless you know how to turn it into joy.

Make today a happy day!

CONTACTING KENFORD NEDD, M.D.

DR. KENFORD NEDD IS AN INTERNATIONAL SPEAKER who inspires innovation, creativity, and professional effectiveness. His keynote speeches captivate his audiences and motivate them to make lasting changes as he brings people more fully to their lives and work.

From his years of private practice in family and behavioral medicine, involving biofeedback and relaxation therapy, Dr. Nedd has developed effective strategies for personal and professional enrichment. As a graduate of Dalhousie University Medical School, an active member of the Canadian Medical Association, the American Headache Society, and the International Headache Society, Dr. Nedd brings a solid understanding of human physiology to his work.

Dr. Nedd has been the host of the television show "Changes," and had a weekly guest spot on the CBC network. He also hosts "Two Minutes with Ken Nedd," a radio program syndicated around the world.

Dr. Nedd consistently receives the highest marks from his audiences. He has been featured as one of the top ten speakers in the journal of the American Society of Association Executives.

To bring Dr. Nedd to your next seminar or meeting, contact **info@stressdoctors.com** or call 604.632.9500.